Stop Chasing Carrots

Chris Masi

ISBN-10:
1533227683

ISBN-13:
978-1533227683

For my dad.

Contents

Contents   5

Part 1: Creating a scientifically sound philosophy of life

Introduction   1

The fundamental problem with self-help   5

What makes us happy?   12

Can we become anything we want?   26

How does our mind work?   34

Why we do what makes us unhappy   46

Why it is hard to let go   52

What do we want from life?   61

How to live our true selves despite our limitations   70

How to stop doing what hurts us   83

Part 2: Applying our philosophy of life

How to develop our talents   91

How can we show more self-control?   97

Do we need self-esteem to lead good lives?   104

How to evaluate ourselves reasonably   113

Should we ignore what others think of us?   120

How to know what to believe   129

Does success leave clues?   142

How can we stop self-sabotage?   148

Do our thoughts influence reality?   152

How to make better decisions   158

Conclusion   171

10 rules for a good, happy life   175

Introduction

As I write these lines, I am sitting in the Eagle's Nest, a restaurant atop the summit of Mount Kehlstein in the Bavarian Alps. Originally built as a gift for Adolf Hitler's 50th birthday, places like this remind us of the horrific consequences unreflective ideologies and faulty logic can have. More than 40 million people died because Adolf Hitler followed his dream, ignored the naysayers, and everybody in Germany believed him. Strangely enough, modern self-help books encourage us to follow a similar path. They want us to define a dream, ignore all doubters, and never relent. While this approach doesn't necessarily transform us into dictators, it makes our lives equally empty, cold, and unhappy. To lead good, happy lives, we need to overcome the self-help deceptions that have spread throughout our society. This book will identify these myths, show why they are hurtful, and replace them with a philosophy of life that can generate happiness and fulfillment. Our approach will be entirely based on scientific research.

Why you should read this book

This book attempts to solve the fundamental dilemma we face when we read books on how to lead a good life. Self-help books contain many fancy concepts, lots of lofty promises, and endless amounts of well-sounding strategies – but often little actual content. The ideas in these books are mostly based on wishful thinking and faulty logic, not on facts and research. On the other hand, there are highly scientific books, based on sophisticated research and hard facts, containing all the knowledge anyone could ever need to become happy and fulfilled – but these books package their knowledge in too complicated a manner for most people. With this book, we will combine the best of both worlds – the fact-driven insight of scientific studies and the readily comprehensible nature of self-help books. We will overcome the myths currently surrounding happiness and a good life and replace them with knowledge and wisdom. We will base our analysis on scientific research and psychological studies, but we will try to put the results in terms that are as easy to understand as a self-help book.

This book is not exclusively for those who have read self-help books before. It is for all those who:

- … are fed up with predefined happiness ideas.
- … are unfulfilled, but do not know why.

- … found that their achievements left them unfulfilled.
- … wonder what to do with their lives, what could make them happy.
- … want to make the most of their abilities while avoiding unrealistic promises.
- … want to face their limitations realistically – without ignoring them but also without giving up on who they are.

Even if you have never read a single self-help book in your life, you have been in contact with most of the misconceptions propagated by them. They are a part of our society and our culture. This book will show you:

- How to replace self-help deceptions with scientifically accurate concepts.
- How to combine a passionate life with following long-term goals.
- How to avoid the mental processes that can trick us into pursuing what fails to make us happy.
- How to free yourself from wrong beliefs.
- How to let go of the things that make you unhappy.

With these concepts, you will immediately be able to create a better, happier, and more fulfilled life.

Why you should not read this book

This book attempts to uncover the truth about a good, happy life. Because of this intention, there are some things it can't do.

- This book will not tell you that you can become anything you want – you can't.
- This book will not tell you that your thoughts will automatically become reality – they will not.
- This book will not tell you that you can be happy every day of your life – you can't.
- This book will not tell you that there is a law, a magical force, or a higher power that will take care of you – there is not.
- This book will not tell you that something or someone else can make you happy – nothing and nobody can.

This book will tell you that the quality of your life depends on you. While there are some things you can do to improve the quality of your life, there's nothing you can do to make it perfect. If you are looking for a magic bullet, this book will disappoint you. Be aware, however, that these magic bullets are always a lie. This book might not promise as magical a solution as self-help books, but the promises made are achievable and will help you lead a better life. They are therefore worth more than anything ever written in a typical self-help book.

What you will find in this book

This book is not a point by point rebuttal of self-help deceptions – there are too many to disprove them all one by one. This book attempts to create a philosophy of life based on scientific facts and research. Along the way, we will overcome self-help deceptions but also create a deeper understanding of how our minds work, enabling us to recognize and avoid self-help deceptions on our own.

In the first part of this book, we will cover the basics of a good life:

- How can we lead a good, happy life?
- What tricks us into doing what make us unhappy?
- How can we avoid these traps?

Research shows that the pursuit of material wealth and achievements fails to create true happiness and that happiness depends four times as much on why we do things than on what these things bring our way. While most of us try to change our life circumstances to create happiness, believing that we will finally be happy when we have a loving family, a good job, and a big house, these factors have little influence on how happy we are. Studies show that broke, divorced, and paralyzed people are just as happy as the rest of us. Our immense effort to create better life circumstances contributes to a field with little influence on our happiness while taking away from what can make us happy the most – the more we focus on changing our life circumstances, the less happy we are.

Once we have established the fundamentals, the second part of this book will analyze detailed issues surrounding a happy life and self-help deceptions – issues such as:

- Do we need self-esteem to lead good lives?
- What is self-sabotage and how can we stop it?
- How can we show more self-control?

For most of these issues, the answer will not be what you expect. While all chapters of the second part build on the first part and you should read part 1 before you start with part 2, in part 2, you can start with the chapter that intrigues you the most.

This book is the result of more than a decade of study and intense thinking. Whether you want to understand your feelings better, feel more fulfilled, or make sure that you are on the right track in life – I hope you will find this book interesting, helpful, and enlightening; and I hope you will enjoy reading these pages as much as I enjoyed writing them.

Part I

Creating a scientifically sound philosophy of life

Chapter 1

The fundamental problem with self-help

I vividly remember the day I started reading self-help books. I was 14 years old, and I had just bought a book by a German self-help guru that promised to guide me to my first million in seven years. While I liked the prospect of being a millionaire at age 21, my feelings were mixed. I knew that this book was going to open a new world to me, but I doubted that this world was real and whether I wanted to live in it. Back then, there was little I understood about the world, but I was afraid that I might end up one of the negative stereotypes I had heard about self-help.

As I grew older and kept reading self-help literature, my doubts faded. It all seemed to make sense. I started to see the world through the self-help lens, recognizing go-getters and people with limiting beliefs everywhere. My new world divided itself into us, who had seen the light, and them, who had not. Of course, *they* did not understand *us*, but how could they?

Over the years, the ideas presented in self-help literature helped me leave the small East German town I was born in, a town where most people grow old before they ever were young. I completed a college degree, started two companies, became the leader of our university group, held positions in a political party, played first league American football in Germany, became financially independent, bought my first apartment, and met many interesting people – high-ranking politicians, entrepreneurs, former NFL players, and media representatives. Without self-help, few of these things would have been possible.

Nonetheless, even though my life circumstances had changed dramatically, these changes felt empty to me. Self-help had helped me get away from what I wanted least, but it failed to help me find what I wanted most. Naively, I always expected the next accomplishment, the next higher political position, the next higher amount of money I made to bring me everlasting happiness. In line with what self-help books had promised me, I was trying to find happiness through achievement, through changing my life circumstances. The results were disappointing, to say the least. I was just as happy as before, and with all the effort I had put in, with all the nights I could have met friends but sat at home working, with the girlfriend I never had because I was too busy, I felt that I had given up more than I had won – if I had won anything at all.

I was unsatisfied. While my doubts in the self-help doctrine had faded over the years, they never went away entirely. There was always this hushed voice in the back of my head telling me that self-help was pushing me in a direction I was reluctant to go. Something about the premise of self-help, about promising the secret to life never agreed with me. Now these doubts resurfaced stronger than ever before. I knew that I needed to find facts, measurable data, and statistics about happiness and how to achieve it. If these facts backed up self-help's teachings – great. If they did not, I had to abandon self-help. I started searching for all statistics on success, happiness, and a good life I could find; I studied research from psychologists and happiness experts; I devoured everything that was even remotely connected to the topic. The more I read, the more one thing became clear to me: The entire self-help world is built on shaky ground. It commits inexcusable logical errors, encourages us to pursue things that fail to make us happy, and creates shallow, unreflective personalities. Self-help distorts our view of life in a way that hurts us and, paradoxically, makes us unhappier than if we had never read a book about how to be happy.

What do self-help books claim to do?

There are millions of self-help books. They have different names, different catch-phrases, and different sounding strategies. In reality, though, self-help books are like different types of cars. They might look differently and make different promises, but they all work the same way. In the case of self-help, most books are a complicated way of saying the same simple thing: believe in something and it will happen. Focus on the things you want, and you will get the things you want. Focus on the things you do not want, and you will get the things you do not want.

According to self-help books, you should believe in the following statements:

- Focusing on how someone can hurt us means that we will always be in unhappy relationships. Focusing on how someone can make us happy means that we will soon find the love of our lives.
- Thinking that we are little fatties means we will never lose weight. Thinking that we are strong, thin, and sexy means we become exactly that.
- Believing that we are meant to be poor will keep us poor. Believing that we are meant to be rich will make us rich.

According to self-help books, we are as good or bad as we believe to be, our lives will unfold according to our expectations. Based on this principle, self-help books claim that positive thinking, self-esteem, and hard-work are the key to success in any aspect of life. Since we create what we focus on, focusing on the positive will make everything fall into place – a change of focus will inevitably lead to a change in life. To assist us with our positive thinking, most self-help books provide techniques to help us concentrate on positive things: writing statements we read every morning, making lists with positive quotes we work through during the day, and performing check-ups in the evening. When all is said and done, we become perpetually positive, always smiling, over-confident self-proclaimed go-getters.

But does that increase our chances to lead good, happy lives? Will it help us get the things we want, and will the things we want be the things we need? Research says no.

What do self-help books actually do?

Self-help books use what psychologists know as the *confirmation bias*: We interpret information in a way that confirms the theories, ideologies, and convictions we already believe in – we see what we want to see. In its simplest way, we experience the confirmation bias when we are in love. Our belief that our partner is perfect makes us ignore their negative characteristics. We only see the good side we want to see.

Self-help books try to transfer the confirmation bias into our everyday lives. According to their logic, people who believe in a world full of opportunities and in their power to capitalize on these opportunities will sooner or later capitalize on one of them. People who believe that they are not good enough and that something is stopping them will not take action and lead worse lives. Self-help books are trying to nudge us to the better side of this equation.

Of course, most self-help books use fancy names for this simple principle, calling it "the law of attraction" and other grandiosities, but they are just trying to use simple mental phenomena that psychologists have known for decades. Nonetheless, the basic promise of self-help sounds intriguing. "Believe in good things and good things will happen" is something we all can do, which means we all can have good things happen to us. Unfortunately, this promise is a lie. And that is where the problems start.

Why are self-help deceptions making us unhappy?

The confirmation bias can be dangerous. In his book *The Art of Thinking Clearly*, Rolf Dobelli describes an experiment that explains the problem with the confirmation bias:

A professor wrote down the numbers 2, 4, and 6. He then asked his students to find the rule he used to come up with this line of numbers by proposing more numbers that would fit the rule. Naturally, the students started with 8. The professor answered that 8 fitted the rule. The students continued with 10, 12, and 14, with the professor always responding that these numbers fit the rule.

Now the students tried to solve the question. They said, "The rule is: add 2 to the previous number." It's very likely, you agree with their solution, right?

The professor, however, shook his head. He said, "No. That is not the rule." The students were stunned.

Then one student said, "1?" The professor answered, "Doesn't fit the rule." "9?" "Fits the rule." The student continued with 59, -19, 30, 0, and so on. After a while, he said, "The rule is: every number has to be higher than the previous number."

The professor nodded in agreement.

This student was able to see the obvious point his fellow students had missed because he attacked the problem with a different way of thinking. Instead of trying to prove his idea right, he wanted to prove it wrong – he wanted to find *disconfirming evidence*. Only after he failed to falsify his theory, he accepted the logical conclusion that it must be true, avoiding the confirmation bias and finding the truth. The other students fell for the confirmation bias because they tried to prove their idea right. They neglected to ask one of the many numbers that could have disproved their theory; they only tried a few examples that fit it. When there was no immediate reason to discard their theory, they accepted it as the truth – and were wrong.

In this case, the students' mistake had no far-reaching consequences; they only gave a wrong answer in the classroom. If they made a similar error in an important decision of their lives, however, the confirmation bias could have horrific consequences for them. It could send them down a career path they will hate, it could trick them into a relationship they will regret, and it could convince them to make financial investments that will ruin them. That is the danger of the confirmation bias. We only see what we want to see. As long as what we want to see is true, we are in luck. If it is not, we set ourselves up for failure and often do stupid or dangerous things. Consequently, psychologists consider the confirmation bias an example of faulty logic. It causes us to make wildly irrational decisions.

That's where another form of faulty logic comes into action: the *survivorship bias*. The survivorship bias describes our tendency only to study the survivors or achievers, concluding that what they did must be the reason for their success. With this logic, we ignore those who did the same things but died or failed – we elevate coincidental or meaningless factors to crucial elements of success. Combined with the confirmation bias, the survivorship bias can create a distorted view of the world. Some people will get lucky – they will turn an irrational decision based on the confirmation bias into a huge success story. When we succumb to the survivorship bias and only study success stories, we can easily think that believing in a confirmation bias is a requirement for success.

That's what all self-help books do when they claim to have studied 100 successful people and found the common reason for their success. They mistake a common fact for a cause. In reality, the overwhelming majority of all people who did the same thing as those 100 successful people failed. By ignoring the failures, we are likely to become one of them.

Anthony Robbins, for example, recommends a technique he calls modeling:

> *„If you want to be successful, find someone who has achieved the results and copy what they do, and you will achieve the same results. "*
> ANTHONY ROBBINS

In Robbins' words, success leaves clues. By finding someone who already achieved what we want to achieve and copying his approach, we can learn what it takes to succeed. Robbins' theory is a good example of the survivorship bias. Based on his theory, aspiring musicians should quit school and start touring in the back of an old van – that is what most successful bands did. Aspiring actors should drop out of school and move to Los Angeles, aspiring athletes should focus as little on their education as possible and use every free minute to practice. This approach, of course, ignores the overwhelming majority of young musicians, actors, and athletes who never had their big break and whose decision to quit school ruined their lives. By believing in a self-help dogma based on the survivorship bias, we are far more likely to destroy our lives than to make them better.

Self-Help Deception #1: We can become successful by copying what successful people did.

The destructive effects of faulty logic

Self-help's faulty logic can lead to significant problems. In this book, we will analyze each of them in its respective chapter. To understand the most dangerous problem right away, let's take a closer look at what happens when we buy into the self-help deception.

Most self-help books propose two basic premises:

- We can achieve anything we want if we set our minds to it.
- The key to success is a positive outlook and self-confidence.

From these two premises, they deduct other tips: Ignore the naysayers, prove doubters wrong, etc. Recently, authors such as Rhonda Byrne (*The Secret*) have also introduced a metaphysical aspect into modern self-help books. While older publications often said little about why you get what you believe in, Byrne claims that quantum theory proves that our thoughts create a frequency that attracts what we think. While Byrne's theory is obviously ridiculous, it is also dangerous – it makes us infallible. Since our thoughts will magically manifest themselves, everything we believe in is true, simply because we believe it – we can do no wrong. Self-help books without a metaphysical approach often fall for the same illusion. They raise positive thinking beyond any self-doubt as the gold standard for happiness and success. By this logic, even the 9-11 terrorists would have done everything right. They did what they believed in, they ignored the naysayers, and they never doubted themselves.

The fundamental problem with most self-help books is that we need to question what we do and what we believe. When we ignore disconfirming evidence, we lose the power to distinguish good ideas from bad ones. We replace a realistic self-evaluation with the wishful belief that we can do anything we want, ignoring the obvious fact that we can't. As a result, we set ourselves up for failure. Unquestioned positivity will lead us into dead ends, into situations where our actual capabilities are far from enough to succeed. We could end up like the people who embarrass themselves in TV casting shows. While these people might have other talents, being a rock star or a model clearly is not one of them. Even believing in their dream with all their heart will never compensate for their lack of talent. I'm sure that many of these people are the victims of non-reflective self-help books or at least of parents who read them. As a consequence, they end up heart-broken, disenchanted, and publicly ridiculed.

A practical philosophy of life must save us from getting into this kind of situation. While some people doubt themselves too much, we must avoid doing the exact opposite - blindly fighting all doubts. We need to evaluate ourselves realistically.

Self-Help Deception #2: Always believing in ourselves will make our lives better.

How can we do it better?

Currently, there are two extremes of people: the habitual doubters, who allow fear and insecurity to stop them from pursuing even the greatest ideas, and the self-help narcissists who believe that they can turn even the worst ideas into a success. The truth is somewhere in between. Every one of us has talents that enable us to be good at something, but we are utterly useless at most of everything else. The result is a dilemma: a sound philosophy of life has to grant us the confidence to develop our talents while at the same time allowing us to doubt our path.

This goal is not a contradiction. Confidence can arise from other sources than blind faith – we can build confidence through doubt. We need a philosophy of life that actively seeks out disconfirming evidence and uses it to free us from wrong beliefs. When we employ such a philosophy of life, we know that the beliefs that have withstood this thorough testing might still be imperfect, but we can be sure that they are currently the best we can do. They are the direction in which we must move. As soon as we obtain new information along the way, we might be able to improve these beliefs. But for now, acting on any belief that is less than the best we can do would be an illogical decision that can only hurt us.

With this kind of philosophy of life, we can simultaneously be confident and doubt ourselves, combining the advantages of both approaches to act on opportunities and recognize dead ends. That is the kind of philosophy of life we need. This book attempts to create such a philosophy of life based on scientific evidence. Along the way, we will question the beliefs self-help literature propagates, and we will replace anything that fails the test with what we know to be true from scientific evidence.

Conclusion

1. Most self-help books use a fundamentally flawed approach. Among other mistakes, they most notably fall prey to the confirmation bias and the survivorship bias.
2. This faulty logic leads self-help books to propagate an inherently distorted way of thinking. When we follow their logic, we make our lives worse, not better.
3. Overcoming self-help deceptions helps us to create a better philosophy of life – a philosophy that is based on evidence, facts, and what we know about our minds. This book aims to achieve this goal.

Further reading

To help you dive deeper into the topics that interest you the most, the end of each chapter will present you with a selection of books and articles to learn more about the chapter's main points. To prevent you from being overwhelmed with a long reading list, I will try to keep recommendations as short and as few as possible.

Rolf Dobelli: The Art of Thinking Clearly.
A good book to help us avoid faulty reasoning. While the book doesn't include the reasons for faulty logic, it is a great tool to help avoid its effects. An insightful, easy read about our daily biases.

Chapter 2

What makes us happy?

"Our daily happiness depends at least four times as much on how we approach life than on what life brings our way."

MARK LEARY

On January 26, 1997, the Green Bay Packers won the Super Bowl, the final of the American football league (NFL) and the biggest game on the planet. Immediately after the final whistle blew, as the confetti was raining down and the Lombardi trophy was about to be presented, Brett Favre, Green Bay's quarterback and the league's most valuable player for the past two seasons, stood silently amidst the celebration, visibly disappointed. Even though he had played a great game and had achieved what he had worked for all his life, he was not completely happy about his achievement. He had sacrificed his body, his health, and almost his marriage to get to this point, but, as he admitted later in an interview, when he arrived where he always wanted to be, all he could think was, "Is that all there is to it?"

We all have experienced similar situations where we dedicated all our energy to achieving a goal, but when we achieved it, it either failed to make us happy at all or only created a short-lived happiness burst. Self-help books, by nature, encourage us to put a lot of effort into achieving goals, implying that accomplishing these goals will make us happy. As research suggests, this approach is futile. When we achieve what we worked so hard for, we will feel as disappointed as Brett Favre. Let's find out why, and how we can avoid this trap.

Why pursuing happiness is important

Achieving happiness must be the starting point, the fundamental goal of any philosophy of life. Happiness is the one motivation that drives everything we do. We buy things, we enter relationships, and we change other life circumstances because we think that these things will make us happy. We measure every small decision such as what to eat or what to wear by how happy we think it can make us. Aside from our survival instinct, almost everything we do is motivated by our desire to gain happiness and avoid unhappiness.

Sometimes, the pursuit of happiness is considered selfish, something that focuses exclusively on ourselves and ignores the needs of everybody else. This is a misconception spread by people who fail to understand the true nature of happiness. As this book will show, true happiness is always tied to contribution. There is no such thing as doing one thing for our happiness and another thing for the common good. In a good life, the pursuit of happiness and contributing to the common good align perfectly and benefit each other. The more we contribute, the happier we are.

A good philosophy of life must do three things:

1. It must include the pursuit of happiness as our main goal. Any philosophy of life that puts anything but our strongest desire first will fail to have a lasting impact on our lives.
2. It must use our desire to be happy to our advantage – while we pursue happiness, we must automatically accomplish all the other goals we want from life – start a family, have a fulfilling career, contribute to society, etc.
3. It must unite the pursuit of happiness with all our other desires in pursuit of a common goal. While our drive to be happy is stronger than our other drives, to live fulfilled lives, we must not allow it to overrule everything else we want to do.

How can we achieve this? Let's start by exploring what makes us happy.

What do we know about happiness?

For centuries, scientists have ignored happiness as a topic best left to religions and gurus. Luckily, over the past decades, this attitude has changed. While science has not yet found all the answers, it has found a wealth of facts that we can use to create a scientifically sound philosophy of life. Especially Sonja Lyubomirsky, an American research psychologist and author of books such as *The How of Happiness* and *The Myths of Happiness*, has done valuable research on what makes us happy.

When most people think of happiness, they think of someone smiling, laughing, and having fun, someone who is visibly joyful. This momentary sense of happiness is fleeting and doesn't represent what happiness means in the scope of this book. We can lead deeply unhappy lives, but be momentarily happy. As the moment passes, however, our emotional state will soon be back to where it was before.

For this book, happiness means something deeper. We want a sense of fulfillment, contentment, and satisfaction – we want peace of mind, a feeling that we are doing what we want to do and being where we want to be, both physically and metaphorically. To distinguish this feeling from the momentary form of happiness, psychologists created the term *subjective well-being*. To avoid too technical of a language, I will keep using the term happiness, but please know that I'm talking about the deeper, long-term sense of the feeling.

So what do we know about happiness?

Our happiness depends on three factors

While there is a wide array of factors that influence happiness, they can all be subsumed under three main factors:

1. Life circumstances,
2. Genetics,
3. Behavior & thoughts.

To be happy, most of us focus on changing our life circumstances. We want to make more money, find a partner, start a family, become famous, etc. We may never think about the effect of genetics; and if we consider changing our thoughts and behaviors, we do it because we hope to alter our life circumstances. Many of us have tried to think more positively or to increase our self-esteem, but we did it to make more money, be more respected, get someone to fall in love with us, etc. – not because we thought that changing our way of thinking in itself could make us happy.

That's a mistake. Research has shown that our life circumstances determine only about 10 percent of our happiness. In other words: our job and our finances, the size of our house, car, and TV; our family situation, our health, all our relationships, etc. – these things make up only 10 percent of our happiness. In 2010, researchers found that when people who made less than $75,000 per year received a raise, their long-term happiness increased a little. Above the $75,000 mark, however, more money and happiness showed no correlation. Someone who made $75,000 was just as happy as someone who made $750,000. Apparently, how much money we make has little influence on our happiness.

Why is this? It seems that below a certain level of income, we have to worry about money. We are scared we might get sick because we can't afford to go to the doctor; we are scared our car might break down because we can't afford to take it to the shop, and we are worried about bills coming in that we can't afford to pay. These worries weigh on us and reduce our happiness. Starting with a certain income, however, these worries are gone. We can afford insurance, we can get our cars fixed, and we can pay the bills. After we have eliminated these worries, more money fails to increase our happiness. When we have enough money to live a worry free life, more money can only replace what is already good enough with what is more expensive but not better. Economists call this principle *diminishing marginal utility* – our tenth loaf of bread makes us less happy than our first, and at some point, another loaf of bread will not increase our happiness at all. The same principle applies to money; we are just better at shrouding our minds to it.

To be happy, we do not have to make exactly $75,000 per year. We need to make enough to support the life we want to live. Depending on how frugal we are, we might be equally happy with much less money or we might need more. One point that influences our minimum income is whether we want to have kids. If we want six kids, we need more money than if we want none. There is no need to feel bad if someone makes more money than we do. If they need more money to support the lives they want to live, then that's fine, but it is not a measure of our worth as human beings.

Simply put, money doesn't make us happy. Only a total lack of money can make us unhappy. In the same way, other life circumstances do not make us happy – they can only make us unhappy when we experience a great void:

- Five friends make us as happy as 50 friends. We become unhappy when we have no friends.

- Any working car makes us as happy as the newest Mercedes. We become unhappy when we have no car at all or a car that breaks down constantly.

- A house or an apartment can make us as happy as a mansion. We become unhappy when we are unable to afford our own place at all.

- Being average looking makes us as happy as being beautiful. We become unhappy when we look unkempt and smell bad.

Beyond a certain point, increasing our life circumstances is a waste of time and effort. We have to reach a certain minimum in all aspects but we don't have to lead the world in anything to be happy. While most of us think that better life circumstances will bring us a lot of happiness over a long period, they will only bring us a little happiness over a short period. When we think about our life situation, we know this to be true. We tend to make more money as we get older, and we can buy more things. But do these things make us happier on a daily basis? No.

Even on a grand scale, outer circumstances fail to improve our happiness. In the United States and most western nations, the average income has increased steadily over the last decades, even when we account for inflation. In the 1940s, many households had no running water, no indoor toilets, and no electricity. They had no internet, no iPhones, no flat screen TVs, and no high-tech cars; plus there was a World War, and millions of people died on the battlefields. Since then, our life situation has improved drastically, but our happiness has not. Polls show that people in the U.S. ranked themselves happier in the 1940s than they do now. Apparently, life circumstances are not all that important.

These findings should not mislead us to buy into limitless minimalism. Minimalism, too, is a philosophy of life that is based on changing our life circumstances and, therefore, is unable to create happiness. While it is true that most of us could be happier with less, going from one extreme to the other will create equally disappointing results. The key to a good life is moderation. We are the happiest when we create the life that satisfies our needs – having to maintain more will make us just as unhappy as having less. Capitalism creates wealthy societies *because* it allows us to buy products for our wants, not only for our needs. By buying a BMW instead of a cheaper make, we create the excess wealth that allows us to maintain space programs and send foreign aid to poorer countries. There is nothing bad about enjoying expensive things, as long as we can afford them without enslaving ourselves to what makes us unhappy. Not being motivated by money is not the same as not making money, and following intrinsically valuable goals doesn't mean to live in poverty.

Self-Help Deception #3: Changing our life circumstances will make us happy.

This knowledge helps us stop chasing illusions and focus on what can truly make us happy – but it also poses questions: If our happiness doesn't depend on our life circumstances, why do many of us spend most of our time and energy trying to change them? And why do many people think that better life circumstances could make them happy? Researchers have found answers to these questions:

1. We overestimate how much and how long life circumstances will make us happy.

One of the most important reasons we overestimate the value of life circumstances for our happiness is that we overestimate how much and how long these circumstances will make us happy. Studies show that, as the outer circumstances of our lives improve or get worse, the effects on our happiness are only temporary. Improved life circumstances do make us happy, but not for as much and as long as we think. When we buy something new, enter a new relationship, or get a new job, we feel happy. Three months later, however, we no longer spend our entire day being happy about what we bought, our new relationship, or our new job. We have gotten used to our new circumstances.

Psychologists call this mechanism *hedonic adaptation*. We adjust to better life situations and our happiness returns to its baseline. Brickman and Campbell created the term in their 1971 essay *Hedonic Relativism and Planning the Good Society*. In the 1990s, Michael Eysenck, a British psychologist, compared the pursuit of happiness to a treadmill. We have to keep running just to stay where we are. No matter what we do, we can never move ahead. Fittingly, Eysenck called his concept the *hedonic treadmill*.

Researchers have found plenty of examples for *hedonic adaptation*:

- Marriage increases happiness levels, but only for two years.
- The birth of a child increases happiness levels, but only for one year.
- Winning the lottery increases happiness, but only for six months.

Whatever good happens to us, after the initial bump, our happiness returns to its baseline – we are as happy as we were before. Nothing we do to improve our life circumstances has a long-lasting effect on our happiness.

With this knowledge, we can immediately lead better lives. After the happiness boost of a new relationship, a new job, or a new car has worn off, we know that this is a normal process. We no longer have to switch from one relationship to the next in search of an everlasting happiness boost; we can settle down, hold on to good things, and evaluate our situation more realistically:

- We know that anything we buy will increase our happiness only briefly. Therefore, we can stop buying more and more things in an attempt to extend the happiness boost. We can learn to be content with what we have, knowing that these things are perfectly fine, even if their happiness boost is gone.

- Since we can realistically expect how little changing life circumstances will increase our long-term happiness, we can avoid spending too much money on what we hope can make us happy. There is no need to get into debt for a new car that will only make us happy for a few months if we must then pay off the debt by working for years in a job we hate. We can anticipate that the overall result of this equation is negative and that our new car will reduce our happiness.

- We know that there is nothing wrong with us when the happiness of a new relationship, a new job, or something we bought wears off quickly. This process is perfectly normal.

2. We underestimate our power to cope with negative situations

Many people say that they would rather be dead than paralyzed. Apparently, a life without the ability to walk wherever we want to go is beyond our imagination. Statistics about paralyzed people, however, show that they are just as happy as the average person – this even applies to people who are completely paralyzed, having to communicate by meticulously spelling out every word through a computer controlled by their minds.

Many of us have been in situations where something was taken away from us that we believed would be impossible to live without. When we lose a loved one, end a relationship, or have to give up our favorite hobby, it often seems impossible to imagine how we can still live happily ever after. We feel as if we have been robbed of a part of our being. After some time has passed, however, our happiness is back to where it was before. Sometimes it takes days, sometimes years – but eventually, we can make the best of any situation. We often misjudge how well we will be able to cope with negative events. We only see what we have lost, being unable to imagine how we can make up for this loss or turn it into something positive. As a result, we overestimate the long-term effect of negative events on our happiness:

- Breakups and divorces make us unhappy, but only for six months.

- After their accident, paraplegics feel unhappy, but no longer than a year.
- In a German study, participants rated their current and overall happiness once a year for 17 years. The study found that only 25 percent of all people reported a change in happiness, with only 10 percent reporting a significant change. In the long run, the happiness of all participants remained at its baseline.

Life's turning points don't need to create major crises. If we get divorced, laid off, or fail, knowing that we will overcome these obstacles helps us to be happier, to feel less shame, and to feel more self-worth. This simple change can influence our lives for the better.

3. We overestimate the importance of one event

When we think of positive or negative events, we overestimate the effects these events will have on our lives because we only focus on the event.

- We imagine how good we will feel driving a new car, the neighbors staring at us jealously, our friends and family cheering our success.
- We anticipate the exciting things we will do with our new partners while we discover each other's interests.
- We dream about how much respect a promotion would get us from those co-workers who thought we would never make it.

As we dwell on these emotions, we overestimate their importance on our lives. We think that the joy an event will create will be our dominant feeling from thereon.

That's a misconception. When we enter a new relationship, we will feel happy at first, and we will do all the exciting things we dreamed of. In the long run, however, the new relationship will fail to solve our other problems. We will still have trouble at work, the car will still need to be repaired, and we will still worry about our health. Even if we remain happy about our new relationship, these other events weigh on us, decreasing our overall happiness and not allowing our lives to become as perfect as we expected them to be. The same applies to negative events. When we think of a break-up, we only focus on the partner we would lose and the things we could not do anymore. We ignore the friends we would still have, the job we would still like, and the hobby we would still love. Within a few months time, these things would make up for our loss and create happiness, even if we are still sad about losing our partner.

Our genes are the most important factor to our happiness

If outer circumstances do not make us happy, then what does? As studies show, the most important factor to our happiness is our genetic makeup.

Experts estimate that about 50 percent of our happiness depends on our genes.

Our genes influence our happiness in two ways:

1. Our genes determine how many happiness hormones we produce

Some of us have a higher natural level of happiness hormones than others. We naturally feel happier, regardless of other factors. There is not a lot we can do about our level of happiness hormones – they are what our genes define them to be. For most of us, this is fine. As long as our natural levels of happiness hormones are within a normal range, we can easily create a happy life by focusing on the things we can control. Only in rare cases, do people have such a low natural level of happiness hormones that they need medical treatment.

2. Our genes determine a part of our character

Our character traits are partly determined by our genes and certain character traits increase or decrease happiness. Through this connection, our genes influence our happiness through our character. If we are genetically predisposed to be easy going and emotionally stable, we have a higher chance to be happy than if we are genetically predisposed to be irritable and neurotic. As researchers have shown, identical twins separated at birth are more similar in their happiness than other siblings and unrelated people, proving that our genes have a significant influence on how happy or unhappy we are.

Combined, these two effects create our genetic happiness baseline. Life events can make our overall happiness stray from this baseline momentarily, but after a while, we always return to it. If you feel that you have a lower baseline than most people, there is no need to worry. As with most human characteristics, our natural level of happiness hormones follows a bell-shaped curve: it flattens at both ends while most of us are in the middle. Very likely, so are you and me. When we feel unhappier than most other people, our problem most likely lies with the third factor to happiness: our thoughts and behavior.

Self-Help Deception #4: We control our happiness completely.

What we do and think matters most

So far, nothing we found can improve our happiness. Roughly 50 percent of our happiness is determined by our genes, which is outside our influence. Roughly 10 percent of our happiness is determined by our life circumstances, which have no long-lasting impact. With that, 60 percent of our total happiness is beyond influence. Nonetheless, we can create true happiness by focusing on the remaining 40 percent. This 40 percent of our happiness is determined by our thoughts and behaviors: how we think, what we do, and why we do it.

As researchers have found, there are many ways to be unhappy. Happy people, however, are all somewhat alike – they think alike, they do similar things, and they do them for the same reasons. In a perfect world, we could use these results as a blueprint for happiness – "do what happy people do, and you will be happy." Unfortunately, things are not that easy. To understand why, let's look at an example. One of the things happy people have in common is they spend more time with their friends and family than unhappy people do and they invest more time and effort into their social connections. Does that mean that we all should visit our parents more often? No. There are quite a few other explanations for these results:

1. Happy people might spend more time with their families because their families are nice and supportive. This attitude is what causes these people to be happy *and* spend time with their families. Happiness and spending time with family are both effects of the same cause. People with more irritable spouses and relatives might not have such good relationships with their families, which reduces both their desire to be with them *and* their happiness. If these people spend more time with their families, they would very likely become less happy. The same applies to our friends. Those of us with a nice, supportive circle of friends are happier and spend more time with their friends than those with less supportive friends.

2. A reduced desire to spend time with our friends and family could be the result of our unresolved issues. We might feel that we are worthless if we fail to achieve great success in our career, spending too much time at work and neglecting our social life. In this case, unhappiness and a reduced social life are not affecting each other either; they are effects of the same cause.

3. We may start a family or choose our friends for the wrong reasons – out of insecurity, social pressure, or financial motivations. As we begin to realize our mistake, we withdraw socially and become unhappy. In this case, unhappiness and a reduced social life both are effects of the same bad decision. Spending more time with our friends and families won't make us happier.

4. We may be more socially active when we are happy. When we are unhappy, we may feel less of a desire to go out and meet people. In this case, a reduced social life is the result of unhappiness, not the other way around, and increasing our social activities won't increase our happiness.

5. In spite of all this, statistics show that a good social life increases our happiness. Researchers accounted for the problems mentioned above, but people with a more active social life were still significantly happier than those with a less active social life. It seems that we can be happier by

investing more in our social relationships, we just need to find the right relationships first.

While a lot of self-help literature simply recommends spending more time with our friends and family to be happy, the issue is more complex than that. Our social lives might have nothing to do with our unhappiness, or they might even cause our unhappiness – in both cases, copying what happy people do and increasing our social activities will not help us become happier. What matters more than the action itself is *why* happy people do what they do. They do not spend time with someone for the sake of having a social interaction; they do it because they enjoy it - because it has *intrinsic value* to them.

Something has intrinsic value to us when we do it for its own sake and because we want to. When we do something because we want to achieve something else or because we think we have to, it is extrinsic – the exact opposite of intrinsic. When we work in a job we love, it has intrinsic value to us. When we work in a job because of the money, the reputation, or because we want to please our parents, it has no intrinsic value to us – it is extrinsic.

When we copy happy people's actions, we miss their recipe for happiness. Simply spending time with other people will fail to increase our happiness – only spending time with someone we enjoy can make us happy. That is a huge difference. People who feel forced to interact with their friends, family, and colleagues, or do so for another reason aside from that it truly makes them happy, become unhappy.

Self-Help Deception #5: There is a blueprint for success and happiness.

What do these findings tell us? Well, there are two things:

- Having a good social life is a deep desire of every healthy human being. When something is getting in the way of an active social life, it points to a deeper problem, either with us or with our friends and family. We need to resolve this problem because it stops us from being happy *and* having a good social life. Maybe we need to find new friends or a partner we relate to better, or maybe the problem is with us, and we need to resolve our issues before we can have good social relationships. Most likely, we are dealing with a combination of both effects.
- Spending time with friends and family doesn't make us happy unless we enjoy it. In general, anything can only make us happy if it has intrinsic value to us – when we do it because we truly want to.

Social relationships are only one of many essential factors to happiness. We can adapt what we learned from research about social relationships to these other essential needs. They all follow the same basic principle: to be happy; we must fulfill our needs by doing what has intrinsic value to us. When we neglect our needs, it points to a deeper problem in our lives that we need to correct before we can be truly happy. We will focus on our needs later. For now, let's focus on how to fulfill them effectively.

How we can create happiness in all aspects of our lives

In ancient Greece, philosophers such as Aristotle and Plato proclaimed a philosophy of life called eudaimonia. Eudaimonia means to focus on the things that have intrinsic value to our well-being and happiness, the things that we pursue for their own sake and not to get something else. Employing a eudaimonic approach to all aspects of our lives helps us to be happy:

- When we choose a job that we enjoy working in, a job that allows us to contribute to what we are passionate about, it will make us happy. When we choose a job because of the money, the status, or because someone else wanted us to take it, it has no intrinsic value and will make us unhappy.
- When we choose a partner we truly want to be with, someone we love with all our heart, they can make us happy. If we take someone because we are afraid to be alone, because we get old, or because we want to impress others with our conquests, the relationship will make us unhappy.
- When we wear the clothes, take the vacation, and drive the car we want, they will make us happy. When we buy the things others expect of us; they will make us unhappy.

Studies show that eudaimonia is strongly related to happiness. Happy people all pursue things that have intrinsic value to them. In one study, college graduates had to report which goals they wanted to achieve during the next year. A year later, they were asked which goals they achieved and how these achievements affected their happiness. The study showed that achieving goals without intrinsic value did not make students happier. Achieving goals with intrinsic value, however, did. Other studies created similar results.

These studies explain why certain patterns of behavior induce more happiness than others.

1. People who live in the moment are happier than those who worry about the future because they focus on the intrinsic value of every moment. Doing something because we hope it will help us later in life has no intrinsic value and makes us unhappy.
2. Happy people are committed to long-term, often life-time goals. They plan their lives in a way that helps them pursue these goals, which helps them see the intrinsic value in everything they do. People without a

guiding main goal lack this internal compass. They find less intrinsic value in their everyday lives and are less happy.

3. Old people are happier than young people because they focus more on activities that have intrinsic value to them. They spend time with their children and grandchildren, and they have found fulfilling hobbies. A lot of the extrinsic activities younger people do are either taken away from older people because of health reasons or because they eventually get tired of them. What remains in their lives has mostly intrinsic value and creates happiness.

We do not become happy when x, y, or z happens. We become happy when we do things for the right reasons. Doing what has intrinsic value to us guarantees we will make the best of the 40 percent of our happiness we can influence. Since eudaimonia is essential to happiness, we must build our philosophy of life around a eudaimonic approach to as many situations as possible.

Self-Help Deception #6: To fulfill our dreams, we must be willing to do what has no intrinsic value to us.

How can we transform these lessons into a philosophy of life?

Based on the findings mentioned above, many self-help books utter such generalities as, "Savor every moment," which is much easier said than done. Accordingly, the question of how to savor each moment and why some of us fail to savor each moment are either left unanswered or answered with truisms. If savoring the moment makes us happy, what prevents us from doing it instinctively?

When we are deeply unsatisfied with our job, our marriage, and our social life, trying to savor each moment fails to provide us with happiness. As we will see later, trying to savor the moment when there is nothing to savor only makes us unhappy – it shows us how little we have to enjoy. We need a philosophy of life that automatically makes us savor each moment because we are only in situations where we truly want to be. At the same time, this philosophy of life needs to remain applicable, and not make us live in a dream world – it must refrain from requiring us to focus exclusively on intrinsic activities. Once in a while, everybody has to do something extrinsic. We all have taxes to pay, chores to do, and errands to run, and it is impossible for us to enjoy them all. Our philosophy of life can, however, help us set intrinsic goals, and then incorporate extrinsic activities into these goals, thereby making them more pleasurable.

As we have seen, happy people are committed to long-term, often life-time goals. These goals help them see the daily necessities of their lives in a more positive light: they aid their long-term goals, which gives them intrinsic meaning and creates happiness. The engineer who wants to help humanity by inventing a cheap water purifier to bring clean drinking water to millions of Africans might not enjoy the bureaucracy involved with developing a new product, but she will face it with a more relaxed attitude than someone who launches a product to make a quick buck. The bureaucracy in itself has no intrinsic value to either of them, but the engineer has an overriding goal that can lend intrinsic meaning to an otherwise extrinsic activity.

With this kind of philosophy of life, happiness stops being something we need to work on for decades. It becomes something we can achieve instantly by shifting our focus from extrinsic to intrinsic goals. Instead of doing what we think we have to do, what will help us in the future, or what others expect from us, we need to do what makes us happy right now. A good philosophy of life helps us connect intrinsic every-day activities with long-term goals worth achieving.

Most self-help books completely ignore these facts about happiness. They encourage us to change our life circumstances and promise to increase our happiness in the process. Some self-help books recommend to use pictures of what we want to buy when we achieve our goals, implying that these so-called "rewards" will make us happy, arguing that imagining how good it will feel to drive the car we bought with our first million helps us stay motivated and pursue our goals with more effort. This type of thinking sets us up for bitter disappointment:

1. If we never achieve our goals, the fantasy of the great things we are missing is deeply ingrained in our minds. Compared with this fantasy, our current lives feel empty, and we become unhappy.
2. If we do get lucky and achieve our goals, our reward will not feel as good as we imagined, our happiness will not increase as much as we hoped. We feel disappointed and start pursuing the next higher reward, only to be disappointed again. We might waste our entire lives chasing the carrot dangling in front of us, only to find that when we catch it, it was an illusion that failed to make us happy.

When we focus too much on improving our life circumstances, we perform more and more extrinsic activities. We overemphasize the 10 percent of our happiness that we are unable to improve beyond a certain point and ignore the 40 percent where we can make the biggest difference. As a result, we become unhappy.

Self-Help Deception #7: Thoughts and motivations are merely tools for changing our life circumstances but are incapable of creating happiness by themselves.

Conclusion

1. To lead happy lives, we must focus on how and why we do things over what we want to get. How and why we do things determines our daily happiness, at least, four times as much as what we have.
2. Following life-long goals adds to our happiness. These goals give intrinsic value to small activities and helps us to be happy every day.
3. To be happy, we must overcome the mental blockages that stop us from pursuing what we truly want. Sometimes we might have to get ourselves into a different situation, a situation where we can do things for the reason and in the way we want; sometimes we might have to resolve our issues and increase our ability to do what we want. Our philosophy of life must help us do both and decide which one is right in a certain situation.

Further reading

Sonja Lyubomirsky: The How of Happiness: A New Approach to Getting the Life You Want.

A research-based answer to the question what makes us happy. Read this book to replace self-help happiness biases with proven facts.

Sonja Lyubomirsky: The Myths of Happiness: What Should Make You Happy, but Doesn't, What Shouldn't Make You Happy, but Does.

After Lyubomirsky's first book, *The Myths of Happiness* provides a wealth of real-life examples of how to adapt her findings to your life.

Brickman, P. & Campbell, D.T.: Hedonic relativism and planning the good society, in: Appley, M.H. (Ed.) Adaptation-level theory, 287-305.

The influential text on hedonic adaptation and why we adapt to good things.

Robert Kiyosaki: Rich Dad, Poor Dad.

Kiyosaki can help us reach the income we need to be happy without having to pursue extrinsic goals – a good book on financial literacy.

Chapter 3

Can we become anything we want?

„Limits... accomplish something important: they force us to figure out what's important. And if we do not want to figure out what's important, they force us to figure out why."

LEO BABAUTA

Quitting football was one the most difficult decisions of my life. For someone who grew up in a small East German town with only one team in the entire state, playing American football was an almost impossible dream. I knew I'd have to wait until I was 18 and could move out of this town. When I was 17, however, I broke my neck, and the doctor told me that I should never play football. By age 22, I started to play anyway. I made it to the first German league, but compared to the American import players who almost made the NFL; it became clear that I would never be anything but a footnote on the team. After I had torn my ACL for the second time in two seasons, I had to admit that football was not worth the 30 plus hours I was putting into it each week. I still loved the game, but in the end, I just was not made to be a standout first league football player. According to all the self-help books I had read, I should have kept pursuing my dream. While every fiber of my body screamed to follow their promises, I'm glad that I refused. I'm much happier now, and I can spend the time I wasted in an effort without results on activities that I care about *and* that generate returns.

The basic promise of self-help books is that we can achieve anything we want as long as we follow the strategy or secret they propagate. But is this basic promise true? Did I give up on my dream too early? Can we really change who we are? Can we all become funny, easy going, and successful? Is the quality of our lives the result of mental processes we can influence, or are we the product of our genes and these mental processes are set in stone, and we have to live with them as well as we can? These questions are important:

- If we are unable to influence who we are and how happy we can be, there is no reason to try and improve the quality of our lives.
- If certain limitations apply to our character development, we have to account for them – we need to know which part of ourselves we can shape and re-shape. That is the part on which we must focus.

Psychologists framed this question as the nature vs. nurture debate: is our character more influenced by our genetic makeup (nature) or by what happens to us and how we react to it (nurture)?

For decades, the nature vs. nurture debate was a controversial topic:

- In the early 20th century, psychologists argued that our character is entirely created by outer circumstances. Some behavioral psychologists claimed that if we gave them a newborn baby, they could shape it to be any character they wanted. To them, babies were born as a blank slate, and, much like on new computers, they could install any operating system they wanted. This point of view is partially responsible for the surge of self-help books we've seen over the last century.
- Other psychologists pointed to our genes. They argued that our character is predetermined by our genetic code, that there's little we can do to influence who we are, and that our lives run the course our genes have set out for them. From that point of view, self-help becomes obsolete, an attempt to change what we are unable to change.

In recent years, the nature vs. nurture debate has lost momentum. Most psychologists now believe that both our environment and our genes significantly influence who we are and that directing our entire focus to only one aspect is a scientific dead end. With *behavioral genetics*, scientists founded an interdisciplinary field of study, trying to determine how much of our behavior is influenced by our genes and how much by other factors.

Finding the answer to this question is somewhat difficult. Nobody could tell you or me exactly how much of our character is formed by our genes and how much is formed by our life-experience because it is impossible to separate our environment from our genes. Our genes have a certain influence on our character, and our character influences our environment, which in return influences our character – our environment is partially a result of our genes. Experts call this the *gene-environment correlation.*

To find a broader answer to this question, psychologists have used many methods. One of the most successful of these methods studied twins. Identical twins share the same genetic makeup. Any difference in their characters must be a result of their environments. By analyzing identical twins who were separated at birth, we can find out how many of them created the same character traits, even though they grew up in completely different environments. We can compare this ratio to identical twins who grew up in the same environment, and the results tell us how much our genes influence whether we develop a certain trait or not. Experts call this aspect heritability.

> Heritability describes which part of the total variability in a certain characteristic is due to a variability in genes – how much our genes influence if we are smaller or taller than someone else, if we are calmer or more irritable, if we are introverted or extroverted, etc.

- If a characteristic has a heritability of 0, our genes have no influence on differences in this characteristic. The environment is the only determining factor.

- If a characteristic has a heritability of 1, our genes determine 100 percent of the differences in this characteristic. Our environment has no influence on differences in this characteristic.
- If a characteristic has a heritability of 0.4, 40 percent of the variations in this characteristic depend on our genes, and 60 percent depend on other factors.

A characteristic can be a physical attribute such as the color of our eyes, the quality of our vision, or our height, or a mental attribute, such as intelligence, irritability, or open-mindedness. In the context of this book, we are primarily interested in the latter – we want to know which part of our mental process we can influence. By determining the heritability of character traits that promote a good, happy life, we know how much of our happiness we can influence and how much is a result of our genes.

Do our genes control who we vote for?

Let's assume that we analyze identical twins who grew up in the same environment and that there's an 80 percent chance that they either both have a certain characteristic or both have not. In identical twins who grew up in different environments, however, the chance is only 60 percent. By dividing 60 by 80, we get a heritability of 0.75 – our genes determine 75% of the difference in this character trait. With this approach, we can analyze how many identical twins who grew up together are both extroverted, both introverted, or one extrovert and one introvert. We can then compare this value with identical twins who were separated at birth and determine how much of the difference in extraversion is due to our genes. The result is 0.4 – our genes determine 40 percent of how extroverted we are.

Heritability analysis has created some very interesting results:

- The heritability of height in the U.S. is 0.87; in Nigeria, it is 0.62.
- The heritability of neuroticism is 0.3 to 0.5, depending on the study.
- In the U.S., the heritability of political convictions is 0.6. That means, even our values and our economic and sociological views are partially predetermined by our genes.
- The heritability for drinking alcohol is 0.4, the heritability for alcoholism is 0.5.
- The heritability of whether we get married is 0.7. The heritability of divorce is 0.3 to 0.4. Apparently, our genes not only determine whether we get married, they also determine how well we do in marriage.

All character traits ever studied show a heritability larger than 0 and smaller than 1, with most of them measuring somewhere between 0.2 and

0.5. In other words, our genes influence all our character traits, but they determine none of them 100 percent – there are many other factors at work.

Of course, there is no single gene that determines whether we drink alcohol, or which party we vote for. Instead, our genes partly determine how our nervous system reacts to influences. These behavior patterns make up our personalities. By determining whether we have the character traits that favor drinking, our genes partly determine whether we drink or not. This decision isn't final, but it has a significant influence. There seem to be three main character traits that increase the chance for us to drink alcohol:

1. Neuroticism,
2. Extraversion,
3. Tolerance of mental stimulants.

People who are neurotic, extroverted, or like to stimulate their minds (party people, adrenaline junkies, smokers, etc.) seem to be able to use alcohol in a way that suits their personality. Neurotic people could use drinking to calm down, extroverted people could like the social aspect of drinking with others, and people who use stimulants could like the stimulating effects of alcohol. People without these character traits have less use for alcohol and are more likely to be abstinent. Similarly, there is no single gene for how well we do in our marriages. Our genes can create certain character traits that make us better husbands and wives, which increases the chances of a happy marriage: well-balanced, easy-going, and funny people are more likely to be good partners.

> Self-Help Deception #8: When we fail to realize our dreams, pointing to our genes is always an excuse for a lack of effort and strategy.

How do our genes influence our lives?

All our attributes are defined by a mix of multiple genes, influencing our lives in multiple ways at the same time. Genes can influence our lives: directly and reactively.

1. Direct gene-environment correlation

Some of our genes influence our environment directly. Even newborn babies show different activity levels. Some are calm, quietly observing their environment, while others are constantly moving their arms and feet, trying to discover their environment physically. Since these babies have not yet been influenced by their environments, their different activity levels must be the result of their genes. As these babies get older, their activity levels will have a direct impact on their lives. Children with high activity levels will hardly get tired. They are more likely to be outside, playing sports, getting dirty. When they get to the age where they can join a sports team, they have had lots of practice in this sport and are athletically trained from being so active. They are more likely to be better athletes, to get chosen early, and to become valued members of the team. Their high activity levels pointed them into an athletic direction from the start, but their influence reaches further. Children who play sports will meet a certain type of people. These people, who are also likely to have high activity levels and all the character traits that come with them, become their friends and create an environment that strengthens the character traits their genes predetermined.

Calmer, quieter children, on the other hand, will get tired more quickly. They play less outside and prefer quieter hobbies such as reading, playing guitar, or playing video games. Through these hobbies, they will meet a different type of people, people who share their lower activity levels, which creates a different kind of environment, thereby reinforcing the influence of their lower activity levels.

Saying that our environment influences us is an oversimplification. Our genes partly create our environment, which influences us in return. With different genes, we would have been in a different environment and would have experienced different influences.

2. Reactive gene-environment correlation

Some genes do not influence our environment directly but influence how our environment reacts to us. For example, children who are genetically predisposed to be nice and easy going provoke a different reaction from people than children who are irritable and angry. As a result, they create a different environment. For easy going children, interactions with others will be more pleasurable, they will have more friends, and they will enjoy being with their friends. That increases the chance that they will become extroverted – a reactive relationship. Our genes determine what we do and how our environment reacts to us which, in return, influences our character.

Another example for a reactive relationship is the relationship with our parents. They will try to surround us with the things we love. If we are naturally drawn to painting, our parents will try to give us every opportunity to paint. They will buy us an easel and colors and books about painting techniques. If we are naturally drawn to sports, our parents will sign us up for sports teams, drive us to practice, and play with us in the yard. If we love music, our parents will buy us a guitar. In all three cases, our environment reacts to us in a way that reinforces our genetic predisposition. Again, it would be an oversimplification to say that our environment influences us. Our environment sees something in us that makes it react in a certain way, but the cause of this reaction is, at least partly, predetermined by our genes.

What can heritability tell us about our lives?

Our genes partially determine what we are good at and what we are drawn to. This mechanism not only applies to marriage, alcohol, and sports, but also to jobs, hobbies, and a general way of life. While we all share 99 percent of our genes – we even share 98 percent of our genes with chimpanzees – it is the small variations in our genes that make us uniquely well-adjusted for some things and uniquely unfit for others. The cumulated and reinforced effects of our genes point us in a certain direction that we can influence but hardly change completely. With this realization, heritability research can tell us two fundamental truths about our lives:

1. Our genes have a profound influence on our lives

Heritability research is incapable of telling us how much of our character is influenced by our genes, but it can tell us that genes influence every single one of our characteristics.

As we have seen with our example of Nigeria and the United States, the heritability of height in first world countries is higher than in third world countries. This is because there are almost no malnourished babies in first world countries while there are many in third world countries, giving nutrition a bigger impact on growth than in the first world. When more environmental factors are constant, our genes make a bigger difference. As this example shows, heritability is always an estimate, never an exact value. We can only use heritability to compare the influence of genes in a *specific characteristic* in a *constant environment*. While this fact limits the ability of heritability research to generate exact and universal statements, it doesn't limit its usefulness for the purpose of this book. We might not be able to tell exactly how much our characteristics are influenced by our genes, but as long as heritability is anything other than 0 or 1 for a characteristic – which it always is – we can deduct that our genes and our environment both have an influence on us and that who we are is partly predetermined and can partly be influenced. That is all we need to know.

Even if we are unable to determine exactly how much influence our genes have on our lives, we know there is a significant influence. Our genes determine a big part of who we are, how we think, and what we like, pointing us in a certain direction. We can influence this direction, but there are limitations. In the same way that our genes partly determine how likely we are to get married and how well we do in marriage, our genes partly determine which jobs, hobbies, and friends suit us – naturally adventurous people will never be comfortable working as accountants.

Our philosophy of life has to account for these genetic predispositions. We have certain desires, passions, and interests that are a part of our nature, and we must incorporate them into our lives. Fighting our genetic makeup is a futile battle that can only lead to unhappiness. We are incapable of completely changing who we are and what we are drawn to.

2. Our genes only partly determine our character

Psychologists are still unable to explain how our genes affect our character – they are unable to look at some genes and predict whether a child will be extroverted or introverted, irritable or easy going, smart or simple. They do know, however, that our genes seem to have a big influence on which things we enjoy, and that we are naturally drawn to. Their influence on the quality of life we can achieve, however, seems less significant. Our quality of life seems to depend largely on how well we use our genetic makeup. For example, there are certain differences in our natural level of happiness hormones, but there is still 40 percent of our happiness left for us to influence. Someone with a lower natural level of happiness hormones who knows how to live a good life and make smart decisions will be happier than someone with a higher natural level of happiness hormones who doesn't.

We need a philosophy of life that utilizes scientifically proven methods to help us make the most of our genetic makeup – a philosophy that accounts for our uniqueness and helps us translate it into the best lives we can live.

Self-Help Deception #9: We can become anything we want.

3. It is not special to be unique

As heritability research has conclusively proven, we are all unique. Except for identical twins, there is nobody on earth who shares the same genetic makeup. This statement is often mistaken to indicate that we are all special. In fact, the exact opposite is true: if we are all unique, there is nothing less special than being unique. Our uniqueness is not something that makes us stand out; it is a unifying factor. We all share the same struggle to fit in and to turn our unique passions and talents into worthwhile, meaningful lives, which suggests we should also allow others the same freedom. When we mistake our uniqueness as a guarantee for great success or as an entitlement to preferential treatment, we subscribe to a lie. We set ourselves up for disappointment and reduce the quality of our lives. We will expand on this point later, especially in Chapter 15 ("How to know what to believe"). For now, the most important conclusion of this chapter is that we are unable to become anything we want.

Self-Help Deception #10: We are all special.

Conclusion

1. Who we are is the combined result of our genes *and* our environment. Our genes set us on paths we can influence to some extent but are unable to reverse completely.
2. Trying to be what our genes prevent is destined to fail. To live a good, happy life, we have to recognize the direction our genes point us in and make the most of it.
3. A good philosophy of life helps us make the most of our genetic makeup.

Further reading

Michael Rutter: Genes and Behavior. Nature-Nurture Interplay Explained.

An introduction to how our genes *and* our environments define who we are, and how both aspects are interdependent on each other.

Frans B. M. de Waal: The End of Nature Versus Nurture, Scientific American 281, no. 6, 1999, 94–99.

An article about why it is futile to focus on one aspect of the nature vs. nurture debate.

Lawrence Wright: Twins. And What They Tell About Who We Are.

An introduction to heritability research with twins and what we can learn from this research.

Chapter 4

How do our minds work?

When I grew up, I often heard two voices in my head: One encouraged me to do what was expected of me, to go to college, to stop at every red light, and to be nice to people even if they were mean to me. The other encouraged me to do what I wanted, to bend the rules, and to let those who mistreated me have a taste of their own medicine. Whatever I did, I always ignored one voice. When someone mistreated me, I kept quiet for a while, only to eventually let them have it. I either followed every rule to the point or no rule at all. Whichever option I chose, I subconsciously felt ashamed for ignoring the other, always contemplating the road not taken, constantly second-guessing my decisions, feeling that I could have done better.

We all face similar problems. While we find different ways to deal with the two voices in our head, many of us are incapable of compromising them into one voice. We always feel ashamed for not having found the best solution to a problem and search for ways to cope with this shame.

Self-help implies that, of the many ways to deal with a situation, only one is worth doing: the way that pushes us to more success and better life circumstances, while ignoring all doubts and all doubters. As we have seen in chapter 2 ("What makes us happy?"), this approach fails to create the results we hope for. As a result, we have to answers a few questions:

- Where do the voices in our heads come from?
- What do they want to tell us?
- If we are unable to follow self-help's one-size-fits-all approach and silence every voice except the one that pushes us to more success and better life circumstances, can we resolve our inner conflict constructively by integrating the different approaches?

To answer these questions, let's take a look at how our minds work, where the different ways to deal with a situation come from, and how we can deal with them in the most effective way.

Why do we do what we know makes us unhappy?

In our quest for happiness, research psychology, the type of psychology that generates statistics and draws conclusions from it, can only get us so far. Research psychologists measure what we do and how happy these things make us. When they find that activity A makes us happier than activity B, they recommend to focus on activity A. This approach makes sense, but it is much like telling an overweight person to lose weight by eating less because people who eat 2,000 calories a day are skinnier and healthier than people who eat 4,000. While this recommendation is valid, it misses the most important point. Any overweight person knows that they could lose weight by eating less. The important question is why are they incapable of doing it? Why do they eat 4,000 calories if they know that 2,000 would be enough? As long as we fail to solve this problem, telling an overweight person over and over again that they should eat less will not help them. Similarly, we all know that doing what we like to do makes us happier than doing what we feel we must do. Simply telling someone that doing what has intrinsic value to them will make them happier is just as useless as telling an overweight person to eat less. To solve the problem, we need to ask the question why we do so many things that have no intrinsic value to us:

- We work endless hours to get a promotion, but neither the hard work nor the promotion has intrinsic value to us.
- We spend time with people who we hope can influence us positively but not with friends we enjoy being around.
- We stay in relationships because we are afraid of what would happen if we ended them, not because they are of intrinsic value to us.
- We waste a lot of money on expensive cars, clothes, and accessories, but neither these expensive things nor the hard work it took to get them is of intrinsic value to us.
- We take jobs and join clubs to be more respected, not because they are of intrinsic value to us.

There's obviously a dilemma in our minds. While we all want to be happy, we constantly do things that are incapable of making us happy. Explaining and overcoming this discrepancy is an essential challenge our philosophy of life must help us accomplish. To achieve this goal, we must answer the question why we often do what makes us unhappy and neglect what could make us happy. After we have determined the cause of our misery, we can find a way to solve the problem.

Are you getting defensive again?

Sigmund Freud, an Austrian psychologist and the father of modern psychology, developed a structural model of the human psyche that allows us to solve our problem. Freud's main premise is simple. Our life is the result of our mental processes. To create better lives, we need to understand how our minds work, why we do what we do, and how to improve our mental processes. For this purpose, Freud created a simple and elegant model of the psyche that allows for a deep understanding of the mind. This is exactly the kind of model we need.

According to Freud, the mind is split into three parts: the id, the ego, and the super-ego. Each of these parts has its unique characteristics, functions, and problems.

The id

The id (Latin for "it") represents our instincts, urges, and drives, the unorganized part of our personality that monitors our basic body functions and wants to make sure that we survive and reproduce.

The id wants pleasure – now

The id wants to satisfy its needs immediately. Freud called this mechanism the *pleasure principle*: the id's only goal is the immediate gain of pleasure. Throughout evolution, the pleasure principle was crucial to our survival, because the id worked as our life support system. The id wants us to stay alive and healthy, and be in a position to choose a good partner. It alerts us to our bodily needs, helps us react to danger, and wants others to find us desirable. The id communicates hunger and pain, but also fear and lust.

Throughout evolution, the id's requests required immediate attention:

- When we were under attack, the id helped us react to the threat quickly.
- When we met someone we found attractive, the id encouraged us to pass our genes on right away.
- When we were in pain, the id made us solve the problem quickly and be ready to fight off predators again.
- When we were hungry, the id encouraged us to find food right away.
- When we were scared, the id made us hide immediately and avoid the threat.

Those of our ancestors who reacted immediately to the id's requests had a higher chance to survive and pass on their genes. Over thousands of generations, this process created the pleasure principle. Today, the pleasure principle is still intact and influences our lives. When we look at children, especially babies, we can see the pleasure principle in full effect. Everything they want, they want instantly. There's no room for compromise. If they fail to obtain the object of their desire, they throw a tantrum. As soon as their instinctive interest moves on, so does the child. This is typical for the id.

We are born with an id

The id is the only part of our psyche that exists right from birth. We are born with certain desires, for example, the desires for food, play, and love from our parents. These desires are instinct-driven. The id is determined by our genes. Our genetic makeup influences our basic characteristics – how active, how happy, or how hungry we are – but also our mental attributes –

which activities we enjoy, whether we prefer mental or physical work, and what we are naturally drawn to. The id is a direct expression of who we are; it can neither be given nor acquired from the outside.

The id is subconscious

Our instincts are subconscious. We are, for example, unaware of why we are hungry. We do not make a conscious decision that now would be a good time to fill up on the 489 calories we need. We simply get hungry, but are unable to tell where this urge comes from, how much we need to eat, or which type of food would be best for us now. Similarly, all our urges are subconscious. We are unaware of why we find someone attractive, why our back hurts, or why we like a certain type of work – we just do. When we get bored, excited, or sleepy, we can try to rationalize these feelings after they arise, but they arise without any conscious effort.

The super-ego

As we grow up, we develop the other parts of our psyche, the ego, and the super-ego. The super-ego is the counterpart to the id. Simply put, the super-ego is our conscience. It is critical and moral; it internalizes the rules we learn from culture, society, and our parents.

The super-ego as our inner critic

The super-ego evaluates every single one of our thoughts, feelings, and actions. If any of them contradict what the super-ego considers appropriate, the super-ego tries to make us fall in line with its requirements again. It can create massive amounts of guilt and shame and can use these feelings as a weapon to suppress a part of our id.

> *"The Super-ego can be thought of as a type of conscience that punishes misbehavior with feelings of guilt. For example, for having extra-marital affairs."*
> ARTHUR S. REBER

This process can be dangerous. When the super-ego suppresses a big part of the id, this self-limitation weighs heavily on us. We have to invest a large amount of mental energy to neglect our instincts while we endure constant feelings of shame. Over time, this inner conflict develops defense mechanisms which lead to massive problems.

The super-ego's demands often oppose the id

The super-ego wants us to act appropriately and be socially accepted while the id demands immediate satisfaction. These two goals are fundamentally different and often oppose each other. We can witness this conflict when parents raise a child. In this situation, they are essentially trying to equip the child with a super-ego. Along the way, the id clashes with the new rules it is supposed to obey: the child refuses to sit quietly at the doctor's, go to school, or eat the food in front of him, but the parents tell him it has to. The child resembles the id, the parents the super-ego – the conflict between both resembles our mind's inherent conflict. Whenever we would rather stay in bed than go to work or when we would rather eat two entire pizzas than watch our weight, we experience the same conflict.

We are born without a super-ego

The super-ego develops entirely by absorbing rules from the outside. While our genes have some influence on which rules we absorb, they leave enough room to allow for all kinds of super-egos to develop. If we were born in a different society, to different parents, or in a different social environment, we would have a different super-ego, even if we had the same genes. This distinguishes the super-ego from the id: as long as our genes remain the same, our id will be the same, regardless of when and where we are born – a difference that bears potential for conflict. If our id is fixed but our super-ego is highly adaptive to our surroundings, there is no guarantee that our id and our super-ego share any common ground – they can be fundamentally different and might not agree on anything. The same person growing up in ancient Greece or the modern United States would have fundamentally different super-egos but the same id. Depending on this person's genetic makeup, they would have more inner conflicts in one of the two times.

We create our super-ego

The super-ego is the result of the rules we gave ourselves when we grew up. These rules helped us to survive and function in the particular environment of our youth – that is the only reason we have them. The super-ego's purpose is to help us fit in, not to be consistent or moral – not even to make us happy. Some of us learned that it is wrong to have an opinion, that we have to accept physical or mental abuse, or that we are inherently bad. From an objective standpoint, these rules are hard to understand. But if they helped us survive in the environment we grew up in; these are the rules we live by – unless we consciously change them. In history, we also find plenty of examples where super-egos developed contradictory rules. Most of the guards in German concentration camps during World War II were gentle, loving family men but had no trouble helping to kill millions of Jews. Their super-ego had adapted a distorted set of rules from their surroundings.

The super-ego is subconscious

Like the id, the super-ego is subconscious. While we can try to rationalize why we consider something wrong or bad, our final decision always precedes any conscious debate. For example, most of us think that it is wrong to cheat to get ahead, but this conviction arises from an undefined, subconscious definition of what is appropriate. Any reasoning follows the conviction we already made subconsciously. The same mechanism applies to all other rules given by the super-ego.

The super-ego developed later in evolution than the id

In the early stages of our evolutionary process, we did not have a super-ego. The super-ego became necessary when we started to live together in bigger groups. With the id alone, we would fight each other whenever our instincts tell us to, we would steal, cheat, and lie to get what we want – hardly a good recipe for a harmonious society. The super-ego enables us to control our instincts and become socialized beings. We can abide by an agreed set of rules, we can treat each other with respect, and we can establish normal social relations that benefit all involved.

The ego

The third part of our minds is the ego. As we have seen, the instinct-driven id and the rule-driven super-ego are in constant conflict. This conflict needs to be resolved – someone needs to decide what we will do. This is the ego's job. By negotiating between the id and the super-ego, the ego is trying to resolve our inherent inner conflict constructively.

For this purpose, the ego controls our thoughts and perceptions. With these tools, the ego tries to capture reality and to react in an appropriate way. Simply put, as the ego recognizes a situation, the id and the super-ego propose ways to deal with it. The ego must decide which of the proposed alternatives fits the situation best, or whether it makes sense to combine both alternatives. This analysis is based on the ego's conception of reality and its possibilities and limitations – a mechanism Freud called the *reality principle*. Contrary to the id and the pleasure principle, the ego uses the reality principle to adapt to its surroundings. It can delay the satisfaction of needs or find other ways to satisfy our needs.

The process of capturing reality and reacting to it by using alternatives proposed by the id and the super-ego is error-prone. What if the ego captures reality the wrong way? What if the ego does a bad job mediating between the id and the super-ego? Then, our actions would not help us deal with a situation effectively. We would do what's bad for us. This explains the problem we proposed at the beginning of this chapter. We do what makes us unhappy and neglect what could make us happy because our ego is doing a bad job mediating between the id and the super-ego. If we can solve this problem, we can solve the fundamental problem of life. Let's explore how the ego works, why it sometimes makes bad decisions, and how we can help it make better decisions.

Self-Help Deception #11: Second guessing ourselves is a sign of weakness.

Where most of our problems come from

The ego is the origin of most of our problems. During most situations of our lives, the id, and the super-ego are in conflict. The id is pulling us in one direction, the super-ego into another. Often, the id and the super-ego are even split within themselves and offer multiple ways to deal with a situation. The super-ego might want us to start a family because that is what's expected of us, but at the same time be afraid to enter a relationship because it fears we will mess up and others will think of us as bad partners. Constructively compromising the different claims of our id and our super-ego is a tough job for our ego. Sometimes, the ego can make mistakes and lose its power as an effective mediator.

To understand this process, let's start with a simple example. Imagine someone who is in love for the first time. Initially, this is a straightforward situation for the ego, as the id and the super-ego agree on what to do. The id wants to be close to our love interest all the time, and the super-ego is already starting to picture us as respected parents. The ego can easily compromise these two views and starts pursuing our love interest.

Unfortunately, this harmony is fragile. At some point, we are likely to get our hearts broken. Maybe a relationship falls apart; maybe our love interest rejects us right away. Whatever it is, the super-ego, which wants to be accepted, will learn that love can create rejection. From now on, whenever the id falls in love with someone and wants to be close to this person, the super-ego intervenes. Much like a child who touched the hot stove learns never to do it again, our super-ego has learned that love is dangerous and should be avoided. Depending on the circumstances, the super-ego might even start to believe that we are undeserving of love, or that we are incapable of being in a relationship. The id might learn that love means pain and start avoiding it, too. For our ego, these developments make the decision whether to pursue love or to stay away from it more difficult. Our mind's unity has been destroyed, conflicting interests are pulling us in opposite directions. Any decision that our ego makes is likely to suppress a part of who we are:

- When we suppress our desire to find a new partner, we risk living in loneliness, never to fall in love again.

- When we suppress the warnings of super-ego and the id, we risk falling in love with every other person we meet and lose the ability to create a healthy relationship.

Neither option is constructive. Suppressing a part of our personality makes us feel ashamed for having these feelings – we think that there's something wrong with us that we need to hide. As we will see in Chapter 5 ("Why we do what makes us unhappy"), feeling shame is the source of many mental problems and undesired behaviors.

A broken heart is a simple example, but it illustrates the problems our ego faces when negotiating between the id and the super-ego. More complex problems often arise from our early lives. In young children the id is dominant. We are born with desires, but our super-ego is just starting to develop. When our super-ego gets an uneven foundation during this time, everything we build on it will be similarly crooked.

A child's most burning desire is to be loved by its mother. When the mother is too busy with herself to give her child the love it craves, the young super-ego wants to help the mother be happy. In this situation, the ego often tries to resolve the conflict between the super-ego and the id by suppressing the id. The ego wants the child to be less of a burden to its mother, hoping that when its mother is happy again, she will give the child the love it desires, satisfying both the id and the super-ego. For now, however, the id needs to take a step back. While this approach is understandable, the child is unable to solve the mother's problems. Therefore, the child's ego will continue to neglect the id. When this process goes on long enough, it becomes chronic. The child has learned that it doesn't deserve to be loved for who it is, that it has to earn love by neglecting a part of itself. This is a problem. As the child grows up and becomes an adult, its desires remain. Since the ego has learned to shut them off, this person feels constant shame and guilt for what they desire.

To deal with these feelings, the ego will create a defense mechanism. In most cases, this defense mechanism is either:

- Narcissism, a personality disorder where people try to find validation from vanity and through achievements, or
- Codependency, the exact opposite of narcissism, a personality disorder where people are overly passive or engage in chronic caretaking.

In both cases, the person excessively relies on others for approval and identity. The ego repeats what it "learned" from the dysfunctional relationship to the mother – it thinks that it doesn't deserve to be loved for who it is and tries to earn love – the person has created a false self.

A false self is the sum of our defense mechanisms. Living a false self means doing what has no intrinsic value to us because we neglect a part of who we are. Since doing what has intrinsic value to us is essential to happiness, living a false self is strongly connected to unhappiness.

By encouraging us to suppress our fears and doubts, self-help creates a false self, too, starting us down a road that will inevitably lead to unhappiness.

Modern brain scans have confirmed this function of our brain. The amygdalae, which are a part of the limbic system of our brains, do indeed store emotion memories and recall them when we are in a similar situation. These emotion memories remain subconscious, but they have a strong influence on how we feel, limiting our possible actions and strongly influencing our memories, our decision-making, and our emotional reactions. Psychologists speak of so-called amygdala scripts that predefine our behavior in a certain way. While these findings are highly interesting, for the purpose of this book and everyday interactions, we do not need to know the exact part of our brain that executes a certain process. Freud's structural model is ideal to understand how our minds work. If you want to learn more about amygdala scripts, I recommend Timothy B. Stokes excellent book *What Freud didn't know* (for details, see the *further reading* section of this chapter).

How to resolve conflicts between the id and the super-ego in a healthy way

To avoid the problems self-help creates, we have to resolve our inherent inner conflict constructively. This is difficult. Many of the events that make us create a false self happen when we are too young to do anything about them, often even too young to remember them. Problems arise from the relationship to our parents when we were babies or young children, or from our relationship to people who played a similar role as our parents. We were ignored, rejected, or made fun of. We felt ashamed for a part of ourselves, neglected this part, and created defense mechanisms. Other events happen later in life. We might have a dramatic love relationship or problems with our teachers, sports coaches, bosses, or friends. To deal with these events, our ego can suppress a part of our id or our super-ego and create a false self. Unfortunately, it is impossible to examine every single defense mechanism in this book, as there are millions of highly complex possibilities, each of them deserving of its own book. The bottom line, however, is always the same. While defense mechanisms once helped us deal with a problem, they now hurt us in every new situation we encounter. To be happy, we have to overcome our defense mechanisms; we have to help our ego find its way back to our true selves.

Living our true self means doing what has intrinsic value to us, to accept who we are, and to not suppress a part of ourselves. Our true self is the result of our genetic makeup and our life experiences.

To understand how we can live our true self, let's go back to our example of heartache and love. For a healthy attitude towards relationships, we need to resolve the conflict between the different directions in which our minds are pushing us without suppressing either direction completely. The ego can resolve this conflict by interpreting our partial resentment towards love and relationships as a warning. When the id falls in love the next time and wants to be with our love interest all day, the ego knows that there is no need to shut down this desire completely, it can be regulated. This way, the ego can stop us from rushing into things and help us determine whether someone is a good fit for us before we enter a relationship, constructively combining all aspects of our mental process and finding a reasonable, helpful solution. This is our true self.

Later in the process, when we inevitably start to recognize the first faults in our love interest, our super-ego might want us to run away to avoid rejection while the id wants to ignore these faults. A healthy ego refuses to submit to either claim. It can use past experiences to judge deliberately whether our love interest's faults will be a problem in a relationship or not, and react accordingly. Once again, the ego has resolved the conflict between the super-ego and the id constructively – a sure sign of our true self. This process, weighing all alternatives and compromising them reasonably, might sound simple, but many of us are torn between both options, always either running away or idealizing someone, and always getting hurt in the process. In our subconscious despair, we often let looks decide whether to run or ignore a person's faults, which is also a false self.

Again, this is a simple example. More complex issues are harder to resolve. Think of the example with the neglected child that grows up to become a narcissist or a codependent. These conflicts often arise from childhood experiences too early for us to remember. If we are unable to remember what caused a problem, how are we supposed to solve it? We can only resolve our ego's problems by understanding them. We need to comprehend what caused our problem, why it hurts us now, and how it stops us from living the life we truly want to live. Then, we can equip our ego with the tools to become a more effective mediator again and find a way back to our true selves.

Without the right knowledge and a lot of self-reflection, this is difficult. Knowledge and self-reflection can help the ego become a better mediator, make better decisions, and, as a result, create a better life. Unfortunately, most of us lack this knowledge and are far too busy and distracted to reflect on our lives. By reading this book, you have found the knowledge you need, which is a great first step. Eliminating your defense mechanisms will increase your quality of life more than anything else. Later, we will focus on techniques for how to do that.

The concept of a true self strongly relates to the philosophy of existentialism. To learn more about the philosophical implications of this concept, I suggest the works by great existentialist writers such as Søren Kierkegaard and Jean-Paul Sartre. Alternatively, there are plenty of general introductions to existentialism, ranging from Christopher Panza's light-hearted *Existentialism for Dummies* to Thomas Flynn's *Existentialism: A Very Short Introduction* and Sarah Bakewell's *At the Existentialist Café: Freedom, Being, and Apricot Cocktails with Jean-Paul Sartre, Simone de Beauvoir, Albert Camus, Martin Heidegger, Maurice Merleau-Ponty and Others.*

Love the conflict

While our inherent inner conflict can cause problems, it is not inherently bad. In fact, we need this conflict to make good decisions and to survive. Much like a just court system uses a prosecutor and a defender to present alternative views of the defendant's involvement in a crime while a judge weighs both options and comes up with a final verdict, our minds need different options on how to react to a situation. The super-ego and the id are our mind's prosecutor and defender – they present both extremes for how to deal with a situation. Like the judge, the ego can weigh both alternatives and come up with a good compromise. Without this system, we would always react in the same way; we would be unable to adapt and grow. In other words: our inherent inner conflict is inherently good. We just need to manage it correctly.

Self-Help Deception #12: We should suppress doubts about the way we are on and continue as if nothing had happened.

Conclusion

1. Our minds consist of three parts: the subconscious id (our urges, needs and desires), the unconscious super-ego (our conscience, rule-giver, and inner critic), and the conscious ego (the mediator between the id and the super-ego), which is trying to capture reality and find the best way to adapt from the alternatives presented by the id and the super-ego.
2. The id and the super-ego are often in conflict. This is perfectly normal and helps us lead better lives.
3. Certain events can cause the ego to suppress parts of the id or the super-ego with feelings of shame. Since neither the super-ego nor the id can self-destroy, we experience this shame for the rest of our lives.
4. To reduce the shame we feel, the ego creates defense mechanisms. These mechanisms trick us into doing extrinsic activities and make us unhappy.

Further reading

James Strachey: Civilization and Its Discontents.

The complete works of Sigmund Freud. A great read for anyone who wants to understand how our minds work and why we do what we do. Some of Freud's ideas are outdated (e.g., the Oedipus complex), but his central concept is still very much valid.

Steven Pinker: How the Mind Works.

An overview of the latest research on how the mind works presented as a collection of funny, informative anecdotes and insightful stories.

Seymour Fisher & Roger P. Greenberg: Freud Scientifically Reappraised: Testing the Theories and Therapy.

A review of studies on Freud's theories, proving the scientific soundness of his structural model of the mind and the theory of defense mechanisms.

Anna Freud: The Ego and the Mechanisms of Defence.

Sigmund Freud's daughter's groundbreaking book on how the ego defends itself against unwanted desires. Ideal for anyone who wants to understand this process in detail.

Arthur Couch: Anna Freud's Adult Psychoanalytic technique. A defense of classical analysis, International Journal of Psychoanalysis, 76, 153-171, 1995.

Similar to the Fisher & Greenberg book, but shorter, Couch's text reaches a similar conclusion. Ideal for those who prefer an article to a book.

Timothy B. Stokes: What Freud Didn't Know: A Three-Step Practice for Emotional Well-Being through Neuroscience and Psychology.

By updating Freud's theories with insights generated by modern brain scans and by strongly relying on amygdala scripts, Stokes creates an easy 3-step process to solve the problems our mental processes create. A great book if you want to learn more about how modern medicine has validated Freud's theories and which anatomic parts of our brain execute which function in Freud's model.

Chapter 5

Why we do what makes us unhappy

"Problems aren't the problem; coping is the problem."
VIRGINIA SATIR

In a football game in my early 20s, one of our defensive linemen suffered a spleen injury. As he wanted to get back into the game, our team doctor told him that he could try, but that he was too weak to make it onto the field. The lineman started running back on anyway, barely made it to the sideline, and collapsed. He had to be rushed to the hospital. What intrigued me about this incident was that, off the football field, this lineman played it safe. He had a safe job and invested his money in the safest way possible, always saying that his number one priority in life was not to be broke. As he was rushed to the hospital because he had tried to play through a serious injury to one of his inner organs, I thought to myself that I would rather be broke than dead.

I knew a lot of football players who gladly accepted risks, on the field and off. They were risk takers at the core of their being and every aspect of their lives reflected that – they had crazy career plans, dangerous hobbies, and risky lifestyles. Some players, however, seemed to use their recklessness on the field as a replacement for what they were missing off the field. These players said things like, "I have to shut up and sit down all week. On the football field, I can finally let it all out." The deeper psychological implication of statements like these kept me wondering for years – why did these players do what had no intrinsic value to them (ruining their health) to make up for something else that had no intrinsic value to them (their jobs, maybe their social lives)? More importantly, why do most of us have equally destructive defense mechanisms?

Self-help has little to offer to answer these questions. While most self-help books encourage us to pursue what we want, they never differentiate between motivations, implying that all our goals are equally worth achieving. Since we have already seen that only intrinsic goals add to our quality of life, we know that this is a misconception. If extrinsic goals fail to make us happy, we, therefore, have to explain why we sometimes pursue them nonetheless. Let's shed light on this subconscious process.

We can explain this mystery with Freud's structural model of the mind. According to Freud, when our ego suppresses a part of the true self, this has far reaching consequences. To understand this process, let's look at an example: an active, adventurous woman works as an accountant in a law firm – a job she hates because it has no intrinsic value to her, and that she only took because her parents wanted her to. How would her mind deal with this situation? Very likely, her id would tell her to get up, go outside, and do something exciting. Her super-ego, on the other hand, would want her to sit down and do a good job – that is what's expected of her. For the ego, the id's and the super-ego's points of view are difficult to compromise. It is hard to see how her id could ever find pleasure in doing such a dry job, or how her super-ego could justify taking two sick days each week to go camping. Probably the only possible constructive solution for this woman would be to quit her job as an accountant and find a career that better suits her adventurous character.

This is a difficult decision to make. The woman's super-ego can probably name plenty of reasons why she should stay in her current job – after all, she has bills to pay, there's no guarantee that she can establish a new career, and who knows what the neighbors will think if she has to sell the BMW to go chase a dream? In this situation, the super-ego can make a very convincing argument to ignore the id – it seems safer and easier just to keep working as an accountant. It will fail to make the woman happy, but that is not the super-ego's concern.

Should this woman's ego decide to resolve the conflict by ignoring the id, she will run into problems. She will always have a desire for adventure, regardless of how hard she tries to ignore it. As long as she is stuck in a numbing routine, her ego has to make her feel ashamed for it. Shame is the only effective argument against otherwise reasonable thoughts.

Over time, constant guilt and shame will weigh hard on our accountant, which will create a deep inner void. In an attempt to find an alternative source for adventure, her ego could come up with the craziest ideas: many people start cheating on their partners even though they love them – they search for adventure with an affair. Internet sites that offer contacts for affairs know this and use "adventure" as one of their main points in advertising – which is ridiculous, but speaks to a repressed need in many of us. Other people pick up dangerous hobbies. They put on wing-suits and jump off buildings; they risk their lives in any way possible. The recent hype for obstacle races such as Tough Mudder has similar origins. People pay a lot of money to wade through mud – something they could do for free in the woods. The woods, however, have no clever marketing that promises a release for a suppressed need. Finally, some people start playing football. This explains the lineman who put safety first in every aspect off the field but risked his life in a meaningless game. Football was his replacement for the adventure, the danger he was suppressing in every other aspect of his life, attempting to fit in.

Self-Help Deception #13: It is perfectly okay to focus on what it takes to be successful and construct outlets for our other needs around our professional lives.

Why are replacements destructive?

While, at first glance, finding a replacement for suppressed desires might seem like a good idea, it is not. Replacements are incapable of restoring what we suppress – which is why I call them *false replacements*.

A false replacement is an attempt to satisfy a need we have suppressed in another aspect of our lives. This type of replacement fails to create the desired result, only making the problem worse.

We can create false replacements in reaction to all kinds of events. As we have seen, narcissists feel that they are never good enough, that they are undeserving of being loved for who they are. They try to find love through accomplishments; they want to be better than anybody else, hoping that they will finally deserve to be loved when they do great things. As a consequence, narcissists excessively search for validation through others – it is their replacement for the validation they lack from themselves. This replacement fails to create the desired result. Many narcissists work so hard that they become highly successful, but regardless of how much validation they receive from the outside, they find it impossible to fill the void that was created from the inside.

We can only solve a problem by eliminating its source. Narcissists can only solve their problem by understanding where it came from and by finding a better way for their ego to deal with it. Similarly, alcoholics and other addicts fail to stay clean if they avoid the personal growth necessary to eliminate the mental need for the drug.

In our daily lives, we face a similar problem: when we create a false replacement, we hope that it can help us live a part of our true selves that we suppress in some other form. We give up on something that is intrinsically rewarding in favor of something that is not. Since only intrinsic activities can create long-term happiness, we are left with an unrewarding activity and an unsatisfied need. To compensate for this lack of happiness and to satisfy our need, we try to find a similar activity to fill our void – an inadequate strategy that fails to attack the problem at its source. The replacement is not what we truly want either, which means it, too, has no intrinsic value to us. As an extrinsic activity, it will only add to our unhappiness. In many ways, creating a false replacement for a suppressed part of our true self is like a lung cancer survivor who refuses to stop smoking but will start eating healthy – it ignores the problem and, therefore, fails to solve it.

There is, however, an even bigger problem with false replacements. Instead of reducing the void we feel from an unsatisfied need, they increase it. In an attempt to find love through accomplishments, narcissists harden themselves and ignore those parts of their personality that they consider weak and unlovable. With this process, they ignore that love is always freely given, never earned. Regardless of what we do, people either love us for who we are, or they do not truly love us. For narcissists, the only way to find true love would be to understand the futility of their approach. They need to grow healthy self-love for all of their character traits. When they learn to experience love from within, they can stop searching for it without. Then, they can accept unearned love from others, and no longer expect others to earn love the same way they tried to do – they learn to give love freely. To find what they are missing, narcissists have to let go of their false replacements and find the way back to their true selves.

Self-Help Deception #14: We can find love & admiration through achievements.

In any aspect of our lives, the only way to find what we truly want is to let go of our false replacements. The entire concept of trying to find what we lack in one area in a different area is fundamentally flawed. It will not work; it will make things worse. This effect exists beyond deep psychological issues such as narcissism; we can also find it in our daily lives:

- When we try to compensate for a boring job by taking up an exciting hobby, our job will feel more boring.
- When we try to fill a lack of significance by buying expensive cars, clothes, and accessories, we confirm that we are worthless without these things.
- When we try to replace a sense of fulfillment by fleeing into more work, our lack of purpose becomes more apparent.
- When we try to fill a lack of love by sexual conquest, we confirm that we are mere sex objects and feel empty and alone.
- When we try to compensate for a lack of significance by overemphasizing our affiliation to a certain race, country, ideology, religion, or sports team, we affirm that we, as individuals, are meaningless.

There are plenty of more examples in our daily lives, but they all work the same way. False replacements are the origin of most of our pain and suffering. We can eliminate false replacements by eliminating their source, thereby enabling us to be happy and satisfy our needs in the way our true self desires.

How to avoid the vicious cycle

False replacements are the ego's attempt to fulfill the needs it fails to fulfill in their original way. As we have seen, however, false replacements are incapable of creating the desired results. The ego notices that, too. Since it failed to solve the original problem, it still feels the same void. This realization creates more problems. In this regard, the mind works in a simple way. It knows which needs it wants to satisfy and whether those needs are satisfied or not. If so, great. If not, it will increase its efforts to satisfy them. False replacements are unable to satisfy the needs they are supposed to appease, which is why the ego can only try to improve our situation by creating another false replacement. This false replacement will fail as well, so the ego will create another. And then another, and then another, and so on.

For most of us, this vicious cycle has dominated our minds for years. We have always tried to find what we are missing in any place other than where we lost it. Now our whole lives are made up of false replacements. There's something missing, there's a lack of purpose and growth, and we know that nothing we currently do can change this. Unfortunately, most of us deal with these feelings by creating another false replacement instead of finding our true selves.

German sociologist Theodor Adorno focused on this problem extensively, arguing that how we spend our free time says a lot about our lives. According to Adorno, spending our free time taking our minds off our lives points to a deep disconnect from the things that matter most to us. Adorno saw free time as a chance to indulge in our passions, to expand and develop ourselves. Instead of focusing on short-term distraction, Adorno wanted us to acquire the tools that help us become better people and create a better world, the tools that will enable us to contribute to the values we are passionate about. Adorno would have encouraged us to stop reading semi-pornographic books and watching mindless comedies, and to start reading about philosophy and politics and watching movies that help us to better understand ourselves and our relationships. Adorno realized that, instead of pursuing the things we want, we watch commercials that connect products to the things we want, then buy the products and neglect our desires – we create a false replacement. As a result, we enter the vicious cycle and remain in our self-created prisons all our lives.

Another reason for the vicious cycle is what Leon Festinger called *cognitive dissonance*. When we do what contradicts our beliefs, our minds must explain this discrepancy. For example, when a parent slaps their child even though they believe that slapping a child is wrong, they often excuse their actions by saying, "I was stressed." In reality, though, this parent was just as stressed as on many other days when they did not slap their child. Stress is an excuse. Our minds invent it to explain why we act against our beliefs – a clear false replacement. When we go back one step, we find that the slap was a false replacement in itself, an attempt by the parent to make up for a lack of control over their child, for a lack of parenting skills, and for unrealistic expectations. These feelings hurt all of the parent's needs:

- Certainty ("I'm a good parent."),
- Possibility ("I can raise my child well."),
- Love/connection ("My child wants to please me."),

- Significance ("My child does what I say.").

The slap is an attempt to force the child to fulfill the parent's needs. To justify this false replacement, the parent creates another false replacement: stress. From now on, their minds will interpret their life circumstances in a way that helps them keep this false replacement alive – the parent will see reasons to be stressed everywhere. To deal with the stress, they will invent another false replacement. Maybe they will start drinking; maybe they will get angry at their boss. In any case, the parent has made their life worse.

Instead of inventing more false replacements that hurt us, we can lead better, happier lives by analyzing and eliminating the original problem that caused the first false replacement. In this case, this would require the parent to work on their parenting skills and reevaluate their unrealistic expectations – a much better approach than complaining about stress.

Conclusion

1. When we suppress parts of who we are, we do what has no intrinsic value to us and become unhappy.
2. To deal with the unhappiness and the needs we suppress, we create false replacements that are supposed to help us live the part of ourselves we shut off.
3. False replacements are not intrinsically rewarding to us either. They only add to our unhappiness. As our needs remain unsatisfied, our inner void grows, and we continuously create new false replacements.
4. We can only escape this vicious cycle by eliminating our false replacements and living our true selves again.

Further reading

Joseph Burgo: Why Do I Do That? Psychological Defense Mechanisms and the Hidden Ways They Shape Our Lives.

Psychologist Joseph Burgo explains how our subconscious mental process creates defense mechanisms, how we can recognize our defense mechanisms, and how we can overcome them. A good read for everyone who wants to get to the bottom of their false replacements.

Alexander Lowen: Narcissism. Denial of the True Self.

Psychologist Alexander Lowen details how the rejection of our true selves, of our feelings, and of our desires, can lead to deep psychological problems and unhappiness.

Chapter 6

Why it is hard to let go

"I am a wanderer and a mountain climber. (...) What returns, what finally comes home to me, is my own self and what of myself has long been in strange lands and scattered among all things and accidents."
FRIEDRICH NIETZSCHE

In my early 20s, I was the president of a soccer club that some friends and I founded. Over the years, the club grew, and more and more people joined. As with any large group, there were some that tried to use the team for their own purposes. At one tournament, my best friend got so fed up with this group that he forced me to make a decision. Either those people left or he would. I knew he was right. I knew that these people poisoned our team spirit and that if I refused to throw them out, the team would eventually fall apart. Nonetheless, I was unable to bring myself to do it. Being the president of a soccer club made me feel significant and loved. Even though I felt the impending doom and being on a team with these people had no intrinsic value to me, I was unable to let go of my false replacement. After my best friend left the team, it took me two more years before I was finally able to quit, too. Until then, irrational emotions stopped me from doing what I knew was right.

In our daily lives, we all face similar problems:

- Overweight people know that they could lose weight by eating less, but they keep overeating.
- People who spend too much on shopping know that they could improve their financial situation by buying less, but they keep shopping.
- Smokers know that they could be healthier and live longer by stopping, but they keep smoking.
- People who neglect their family for their work know that they could be better parents and partners if they spent more time at home, but they keep working too much.
- Students who party instead of studying for tomorrow's test know that they are endangering their future, but they go drinking anyway.

Why is that? Why do false replacements have such a strong grip on us that we are unable to let them go, even if we know that they hurt us? And if false replacements have such disastrous effects on our lives, why do we create them in the first place? It is easy to see how dramatic childhood experiences could cause our minds to neglect a part of our true selves, but it is not that easy to understand why many of us consciously do the many small things that make us unhappy on a day-to-day basis. Why do we stay in failed relationships? Why do we work in jobs we hate? Why do we pursue things we don't want? Dramatic experiences are insufficient to explain all of these patterns.

While self-help offers plenty of strategies to help us focus on becoming more successful, it never explains why our old habits are so hard to overcome, instead uttering such banalities as "we get caught up". Failing to explain the problem, such techniques as making lists or visualizing the outcome we want to achieve only provide us with momentary relief but are incapable of creating long lasting change. To lead better lives, we have to create a better model, a model that reaches deeper. We have to identify the emotions that cause false replacements and find a way to feel less destructive emotions. With this model, we can analyze ourselves and eliminate our false replacements step by step.

Which emotions cause false replacements?

The quality of our lives depends on the quality of our emotions – the better we feel, the better we consider our lives to be. When we are happy, when we feel healthy, fulfilled, and optimistic about the future, we are satisfied; when we feel unhappy, disenchanted, and pessimistic, we want our lives to improve. Since certain emotions make us feel better than others, our lives are an attempt to feel good emotions and avoid bad ones. By pushing us towards what makes us happy and avoiding what makes us unhappy, emotions direct our behavior in three ways:

- Emotions notify us about good and bad events in our lives and demand us to focus our attention on them. This focus helps us to deal with the things we need to deal with, to react to threats, and to pursue what's good for us. Emotions work like a magnifying glass that alerts us to what's most important in our lives.

- Emotions motivate us to deal with an event. Every emotion creates a certain urge in us, an *action tendency* that motivates us to react in a specific way. We often refuse to act on these action tendencies, but we always feel them. Sometimes, we refuse to run away when we are afraid, and we refuse to laugh out loud when we find something funny, but we always feel the urge.

- Emotions create changes in our bodies that help us deal with the event that caused them. When we feel fear, our bodies emit hormones and redirect our blood to help us either flee quickly or be mentally and physically ready to fight. When we feel pain, we cringe up and yell or cry, which makes other people help us. When we feel joy, our bodies help us indulge in what makes us happy.

Combining these three ways, emotions control our attention and behavior – we do what our emotions tell us to. Our false replacements are the result of certain emotions, too. We can understand our false replacements by identifying the emotions that cause them and finding a way to avoid these emotions.

As psychologists have discovered, negative behavior strongly relates to guilt and shame. Shame and guilt both arise after doing something that we consider bad. How we react to bad behavior determines whether we feel shame or guilt:

- We feel guilt when we recognize that we have done something bad.
- We feel shame when we think that we *are* a bad person because of what we did.

This difference – whether we think that we behaved badly or are a bad person – results in a very different experience of shame and guilt. Shame is the stronger feeling because it causes self-recrimination:

- When we feel guilt, we want to fix the problem we caused. We want to make amends with those we hurt, undo the damage, and repair the relationship. We feel sorry, apologize, and try to reconcile with those we hurt. Guilt is a constructive emotion, and it is perfectly explainable why we feel guilt – it helps us behave in socially acceptable ways, and if we misbehave, guilt helps us to correct our wrongdoing.
- When we feel shame, we become self-focused. Questioning our identity, shame creates the action tendency to free ourselves from the negative feelings, not to fix the problem. We withdraw socially and focus on how bad we feel, we become angry and direct our anger towards others, we try to disguise our shortcomings, we lie and cheat. When we feel shame, we might make a superficial attempt to apologize, but fixing the problem we caused is only a secondary goal. Shame is a destructive emotion – so destructive that it is still a scientific mystery why we feel it at all.

As a logical consequence of the different characteristics of shame and guilt, researchers have found that people more likely to feel guilt than shame are more moral and well-intentioned towards others. The more likely people are to feel shame, the more likely they are to show negative behavior. Apparently, feeling shame questions our identity, causing us to fix our identity crisis through negative, self-centered behavior.

Unfortunately, nobody is completely immune to feeling shame. We all feel shame, and from time to time, become self-centered, get angry, and act destructively – but to different degrees. Avoiding shame as much as possible helps us lead better lives. Of course, it would be naive to expect us to do everything right – nobody's perfect – but we can act in ways that help us feel guilt instead of shame when we mess up.

Why do we feel shame?

When we experience guilt instead of shame, we increase our ability to lead good lives. While our genes have a certain influence on whether we feel more shame or guilt, there are mainly two types of behavior that create shame instead of guilt, and both are strongly connected to self-help. When we avoid these behaviors, we can improve our lives substantially:

1. We try to do what we unable to do

The leading cause of self-inflicted shame is trying to do what we are unable to do. To understand this process, let's look at an example.

Emotions guide us towards certain actions. Because we sometimes experience varying or false emotions about a certain activity, many self-help books argue that we can achieve anything we want if we brainwash ourselves into associating the right kind of emotion with the right kind of situation or behavior. According to this line of belief, to overcome procrastination, we simply need to associate positive emotions with the task at hand and then magically start doing it.

This is a misconception. As we have seen, both character and emotions are partially the results of our genetic makeup. We have some room to influence who we are, but we are incapable of changing ourselves completely. Therefore, there are certain limitations to what we can associate positive emotions with. If we have a genetic predisposition for high activity levels and an adventurous character, nothing we try will ever be enough to associate working overtime in a cubicle with positive emotions. If that is what it takes to be successful at our current job, we are destined to fail.

When we fall for the misconception that we are unsuccessful at something because we associate the wrong emotions with it, we will try to change our associations. If we fight our genetic makeup, we will fail, just to try harder and harder – and to keep failing and failing. After a while, we will have to assume that the fault is with us, that we are incapable of doing what everybody else can, that we are stupid, lazy, and worthless. This realization will create large amounts of shame. To deal with our shame, we try to cover it up – we create false replacements.

Self-Help Deception #15: We can associate success-guaranteeing emotions with anything we want.

Any philosophy of life that implies that we can do anything we want will have similar results, regardless of whether the philosophy is based on massive effort, positive thinking, or changing mental associations. They all tempt us to do what we are unable to do, setting us up for failure and creating the foundation for false replacements and negative behavior. We can avoid shame by evaluating ourselves reasonably, by accepting our limitations, and by making the best of our strengths.

Similarly, self-help books that suggest that we can be happy all the time also set us up for failure. In chapter 2 ("What makes us happy?"), we talked about two definitions of happiness: an underlying feeling of satisfaction and well-being and a momentary sense of joy. While doing what has intrinsic value to us can generate the first type of underlying long-term happiness, there will always be things that go wrong and make us feel bad – we might get sick, a relationship might fall apart, our friends and family might die. Momentarily, these things will make us feel badly. This is an essential aspect of life, and we should accept it. Feeling good every single day is impossible, and it is futile to try. Any philosophy that suggests otherwise sets us up for failure – we will feel ashamed for not being happy and create false replacements. Ironically, we can be much happier when we learn to accept that, sometimes, we will be unhappy.

2. We do what has no intrinsic value to us

We create shame when we do what has no intrinsic value to us. This process is tricky and sneaky because our initial shame is often directed towards an almost hidden part of ourselves. A successful lawyer, living in a beautiful white house on the hill, driving the newest Mercedes and having a lovely family, might not necessarily feel ashamed for his life as it is. But if this lawyer's work has no intrinsic value to him, if his last couple of cases involved helping large corporations get away with heinous crimes, he might feel ashamed towards the part of himself that wants to contribute to society. This shame will cause negative behavior and lead to false replacements. We create false replacements when we do what has no intrinsic value to us because we are ashamed of ourselves for doing what we hate, for having to put up with a job, a boss, or a social life that makes us unhappy. We think that if we were smarter, more talented, or better in some other way, we would not need to do these things, we would find a solution that has intrinsic value to us *and* could generate the same positive outcome.

Often, these emotions come through back doors and in small doses. For example, when we dream of quitting a job that has no intrinsic value to us, we often invent a long list of reasons why this move would be so inconvenient right now – we would have to move, find new friends, join a new book club, etc. If somebody guaranteed us that we could pull all these things off easily, however, we would quit our jobs in a heartbeat. Therefore, the real reason we neglect what we want is that we are unsure whether we have what it takes to get it. The thought that we might not be good enough causes us to feel shame and creates false replacements.

In our daily lives, we often find ourselves in similar situations:

- We think that we could quit the job we hate if we had more skills, that it is our fault that we have to put up with bad pay, hard work, and a mean boss.
- We think that we could make better relationship choices, deserve better friends, and have a happier family if we were funnier, smarter, and prettier.
- We think that we could be happier, that we would deserve a better life if we were less neurotic, stupid, and naive.
- We think that we could leave our pretty but difficult partners if we were secure enough to overcome the need for a trophy wife/husband.
- We think that we could spend less money on things we do not need if we secure enough to overcome the need to impress our neighbors.

When we do what has no intrinsic value to us, we admit defeat and see ourselves as losers, as someone who is somehow inherently wrong or bad – a mental process that inevitably creates shame and false replacements.

- To deal with a self-perceived lack of intelligence, we try to impress others with our knowledge about a certain topic – even if they are indifferent to what we have to say, and even if we know nothing about the topic. Since we know how clueless we are, we feel more shame and increase the need for false replacements.
- To deal with a self-perceived lack of beauty, we invest a lot of money in clothes, beauty products, and even plastic surgery. The more we invest in artificial beauty, the more we confirm our natural ugliness – we feel more shame and need more false replacements. This explains why cosmetic companies promote a standard of beauty nobody can achieve – our shame is their business.
- To deal with self-perceived dullness, we create social media profiles that make our lives look more interesting than they actually are. Since we know how far our lives are from how we portray them, we feel even more dull and become ashamed of who we truly are – we create more false replacements.

Self-Help Deception #16: Fake it until you make it is a legitimate strategy to create a good, happy life.

Why am I so worried about the future?

The human mind is highly evolved. During its evolution, it has picked up some quirks we have to deal with. One of these quirks can create shame and false replacements in reaction to events that are entirely made up. When we dwell on the past, worry about the future, and create fantasies, we may experience the same emotions and the same negative consequences as in real life.

Many people think their emotions are caused by certain events. This is wrong for two reasons:

- The same event often causes different emotions in different people. When the government is lowering taxes, some people will be happy, and some people will get angry. When we hear a certain song, some people want to dance, and some people want to run away. The events are the same, but our reactions can be very different. Similarly, an upcoming 40th birthday causes great excitement in some people – but in others, not so much.

- Often, we react differently to the same event. When we hear a song we like, it makes us dance and sing along at first, but after a couple of plays, we become increasingly indifferent – the song has lost its appeal, and the same event now causes different emotions.

We interpret events and create emotions according to what we think these events mean for us, even if they are misinterpreted or entirely made up. Psychologists call this the *cognitive appraisal theory*. We do not feel fear because of actual danger; we feel fear because we interpret something as dangerous. Often, we are in dangerous situations without realizing it and are unafraid, much like the passengers on the Titanic, who remained calm for hours while the ship began to sink. On the other hand, harmless situations often make us feel a great deal of fear. During a scary movie, when the hero is about to enter the haunted house, we are often just as scared as if we were actually in this situation, even though we are in no actual danger.

For the most part, we evaluate a situation subconsciously. We are unaware of why we consider something fun or dangerous, and we are unaware of why something scares us or makes us happy. These feelings just *are*. We might not know where these emotions come from, but we all think we can evaluate a situation, other people, and the world in general with reasonable accuracy. If we evaluate a situation incorrectly, even an imaginative one, we still feel the emotions related to our evaluation instead of the emotions related to what really happened.

Most of these self-generated emotions hurt us:

- We worry about the future more than we anticipate good things to come.
- We remember pain more often than joy.
- We dwell in misery more than we celebrate success

Since it is impossible to act on these negative emotions at the time we experience them, they provide no help to us. When we lie awake at night worrying about tomorrow's job interview, there's nothing that we can do to improve our situation. Instead, we will be tired the next day, barely able to think straight, and in worse shape than we would have been without the emotion. That's strange. It's a good thing that we can anticipate the future and relive the past – it gave us the mental capabilities to conquer earth – but why do we have emotions that hurt us? Shouldn't evolution eliminate negative characteristics? And why are all other animals different in that way?

The answer to these questions lies in the evolution of our minds. Our emotions evolved before our ancestors became self-aware. For the bigger part of our time on earth, our ancestors' brains worked just like the brains of other animals – they lacked self-awareness. Unable to picture themselves in a situation they were not involved in at the moment, they had no concept of the future or the past, and they were unable to contemplate what-if scenarios. They only reacted to events they directly encountered.

As our brains evolved, we became self-aware. Since then, there are two systems in our minds running side by side. We can feel emotions, and we can imagine ourselves in situations that are not currently happening – we can picture the future, the past, and made-up events. Each of these systems is invaluable to our survival, but when we combine them, there are some negative side-effects – we feel emotions about made-up events. These feelings fail to help us lead better lives, but evolution is incapable of eliminating their source, for it would have had to eliminate our capacity to imagine abstract situations or feel emotions. Both systems help us more than their combined side effects hurts us.

Can we stop worrying about the future?

There is nothing we can do to stop worrying about the future. We can, however, greatly reduce our worries by doing what has intrinsic value to us. Most of our worries are false replacements for a lack of certainty. When we do what has no intrinsic value to us now, we worry whether all our extrinsic activities are worth the unhappiness they cause and whether we can achieve the result we want – we feel a lack of certainty. By constantly thinking about the future we hope to find something that can give us back our sense of certainty. Since we think about things that are out of our influence at the moment, we will rarely find a magical solution. We become ashamed for not knowing what to do, worry even more, and create false replacements. We can counter this process by doing what has intrinsic value to us. When we know that what we do right now helps us to be happy and to do more of what makes us happy in the future, we gain certainty and eliminate the need for false replacements.

Similarly, dwelling on the past is always a false replacement. When we are hurt or mistreated, we often wish others would care more about how we feel. Even our best friends have their problems and seem indifferent to the magnitude of what happens to us, thereby hurting our essential needs, first and foremost our needs for love/connection and significance. To add significance to these events, we keep reliving them, hoping that others will understand our pain. By feeling sorry for ourselves, we try to satisfy our need for love/connection. Sometimes we might also use the past to justify our present shortcomings. These types of behaviors are false replacements – our true self knows that it is impossible to contribute to what has already happened and that it is useless to dwell on the past.

To stop dwelling on the past, to forgive those who mistreated us, and to forgive ourselves for acting stupidly, we can do what has intrinsic value to us now. Then we can understand our mistakes and negative experiences as necessary lessons in personal growth – lessons that get us into the position to lead good, happy lives now. Over time, this way of thinking integrates past mistakes and bad experiences into our true selves, freeing us from the need to feel ashamed for them.

Conclusion

1. Shame is the most destructive emotion we experience – it leads to negative behavior and creates false replacements.
2. Doing what has no intrinsic value to us and trying to accomplish what we are incapable of causes us to think that we *are* wrong, generating shame and false replacements.
3. Trying to brainwash ourselves into enjoying what we can never enjoy is destined to fail. It is better to do what we naturally enjoy, to find the activities to which we are inherently drawn.

Further reading

Joseph Burgo: Why Do I Do That? Psychological Defense Mechanisms and the Hidden Ways They Shape Our Lives.
See Chapter 5 ("Why we do what makes us unhappy").

Roger R. Hock: You are getting defensive again, in: Roger R. Hock: 40 Studies That Changed Psychology.
A brief overview of defense mechanisms and the scientific evidence confirming their existence.

Chapter 7

What do we want from life?

"The goals that you have set for yourself may be the ones sold to you by larger culture – 'Make money! Own your own home! Look great!' – and, while there might be nothing inherently wrong with striving for those things, they mask the pursuits more likely to deliver true and lasting happiness."

SONJA LYUBOMIRSKY

In my second year of college, I held five different political positions, ran a one-person graphic design studio, was about to start another company with friends, was the president of a soccer club, and I wrote a blog. While I was completely overworked and would have loved to quit some activities, I was unable to decide which one. Somehow, I felt I needed them all and that if I cut one out of my life, all hell would break loose. I neither knew what I wanted from life nor how I could arrange my activities to fulfill my needs. What do you want from life? Can you clearly define what it would take for you to be happy? Research has shown that most of us have, at best, vague ideas of what we want. We want more of everything good and less of everything bad but haven't defined concrete criteria.

Self-help demands us to consider success and admiration as our most important needs. As we have seen, these life circumstances have little influence on our happiness. Instead, our quality of life depends on how our ego is trying to meet our needs. To make this knowledge applicable to our lives, we now need to determine *which* needs we are trying to meet and how we can meet them in an effective way. Without a solid concept of our needs, we will end up in situations similar to what I experienced in my second year of college.

What do we truly need in life?

Over time, psychologists have created plenty of lists of human needs. Since human needs are no exact science, these concepts vary in some details but share a common structure. They define four or five essential needs and two or three non-essential needs, using mostly synonymous names for each need. To keep things simple but accurate, we will use this list of needs:

1. Certainty
2. Possibility
3. Significance
4. Love / connection
5. Contribution
6. Growth

The first four of these needs are essential – without certainty, possibility, significance, and love/connection, we stop functioning as human beings. Therefore, we have to satisfy these needs every day. Needs 5 and 6 are non-essential. We need to feel contribution and growth to be happy, and we will eventually suffer deep unhappiness if we fail to satisfy these needs, but we avoid a mental breakdown *right now* – we can survive for years without satisfying our non-essential needs.

Other models of human needs rename certain needs, for example calling the need for love/connection love/belonging or renaming possibility as uncertainty or variety, but these changes make no difference. Other models increase complexity by splitting needs into two needs, for example splitting love/connection into affection and understanding. For our daily lives, a model with six needs is complicated enough, splitting needs without gaining insight only reduces the model's applicability and should be avoided. For the purpose of this book, the proposed six needs are perfect. To understand these six needs and why they are so important to our lives, let's take a closer look at them.

Self-Help Deception #17: We have a need for success. (The truth: Success in itself is unable to satisfy any of our needs.)

Love/connection and significance

Our need for love/connection defines our desire to feel warm emotions from and towards something or someone, to be connected to a group or an idea. Significance defines our need to be regarded as a valuable member of a social group, someone who can contribute to society and who is taken seriously, treated with respect, and whose ideas are valued.

Significance and love/connection originate from a similar process in our minds. Our ego needs love and significance as a validation for what it does. Our genes equip us with certain desires that create our id, but our ego and our super-ego develop in a blank space. For the super-ego, this is not a big problem; it can soak up the rules from society and our parents. The ego, however, lacks a predetermined set of rules to copy. It has to figure out what's right on its own, using a trial-and-error approach to become effective. For millions of years, this system was perfectly sufficient to guide us through all aspects of our – at that time simpler – lives:

- When we cut ourselves with something sharp, the ego learned that we should stop touching this object.
- When we ate something and got sick, the ego learned that we should never eat this food again.
- When we were attacked by an animal, the ego learned to be careful when approaching this animal again.

For a long time, the ego's trial-and-error approach was fairly fail-proof. Decisions were simple, and we instantly knew whether what we did helped or hurt us. In the confines of our evolutionary environment, the ego was able to create exact, concrete guidelines for our behavior.

In our modern society, decisions have become far more complex; feedback has become harder to interpret, and years often pass before we know whether a decision was right or wrong. In this *delayed-response environment*, the ego has trouble judging its effectiveness. To make up for this disadvantage, the ego uses love and significance as a general indicator of whether or not it is doing a good job. When we feel loved and significant, the ego concludes that what we did must be right. When we feel unloved or insignificant, the ego assumes that what we did must be wrong because it failed to secure our place in a social group. Realizing its ineffectiveness, the ego decides that, as long as it is incapable of making good decisions, it will make no decision at all – the ego shuts us down. We lie in bed all day, cry, and become depressed. After a while, the ego has either found a way to compromise the id and the super-ego constructively, or it creates a false replacement. If it does neither, we stay in our depression and need help.

We always need to feel significance and love/connection through something. If we fail to satisfy our needs through actual love, our ego will lie to itself and invent a way to feel love/connection.

- Lonely people often get pets. Having to take care of their pets and feeling loved in return gives those people the love and significance they desire.
- Some people feel love through self-pity. They think the world has been unfair to them, that their misfortune is the result of their being "too good". This thought process creates a feeling of love.
- Some people feel love towards a sports team and interpret the team's success as proof of the players' love towards them. This thought process also provides a feeling of significance. When soccer fans attack their team's bus after a loss, they are trying to force the team to give them back their lost sense of love and significance.
- Some people become religious and feel loved by a deity and the other members of their religious group.

As we have seen, these false replacements are lies and make the problem worse.

Certainty

Our need for certainty originates from a similar evolutionary background as love/connection and significance. Certainty defines the need for something we are sure to be true, something that we can build a decision on. Our ego needs certainty to be an effective mediator between the id and the super-ego. If nothing is certain, the ego is unable to interpret reality and lacks the basis for a decision.

For our egos, this is a most dangerous state. Throughout evolution, our lives depended on the decisions our minds made. When our ancestors were hunters/gatherers, one wrong decision about how to handle an attacking animal or choosing which berry to eat could lead to death or serious injury. Certain information was vital to our survival. Without certainty, we panic. When the mind understands its decision could endanger our lives, it reacts the same way as in a situation without love/connection: it shuts us down. This explains why people in dangerous situations often act unreasonably – their ego thinks there is nothing it can do, so it enters crisis mode:

- In 1987, the London subway station King's Cross caught fire. There was plenty of time to escape, but many people died because they either were unable to move or because they continued their usual routine as if nothing had happened. Those people lacked certainty, so their minds shut them down. In shock, some people walked straight into the fire.
- Pilots of delayed flights always offer their passengers a new time for take-off, even if they have no idea how long they will be delayed. Without a concrete time, passengers would have no certainty and be more upset than if takeoff was delayed for hours.
- During the cold war, both sides educated the public on what to do in case of a nuclear attack. While tactics such as "duck and cover" provide little help to survive a nuclear bomb, they gave the public a sense of certainty, thereby avoiding a widespread panic.

When we understand our need for certainty, we can accept that there is no absolute certainty, abandoning our self-destructive quest for complete control.

Possibility

Our final essential need is possibility. Possibility refers to the feeling that good things can happen for us, that we can improve our situation, that we can influence our future. Possibility, too, is required for our ego to function. Without possibility, our ego concludes that, whatever it decides, it is incapable of creating the outcome it seeks and of functioning as a good mediator between the id and the super-ego.

In our 20s and 30s, this happens to many of us. When we go to school or college, we have our whole lives ahead of us. We can become anything we want, marry anyone, and live in any city on the planet. Our possibilities are endless. With every decision we make, however, we surrender some of these possibilities. By deciding to study law, we give up on becoming NASA engineers; by marrying person A, we give up on marrying everyone else. Even if we decided well, the reduced sense of possibility can cause us to feel as if we're missing out on something better. Somewhere in our twenties, many of us understand that we have gone from a world of endless possibilities to a life that seems predefined for the rest of our days. We do the same things, work in the same jobs, and see the same people. There's no excitement and no room for improvement; the possibility is gone. For the ego, this is a tough pill to swallow:

- There are a lot of things the ego has put on hold for "later".
- Without possibility, how is the ego supposed to improve our situation?

When we feel no possibility at all, we lack motivation and drive. While questioning the benefit of doing anything, we can hardly get ourselves to leave the house and go to work. In situations like these, many of us withdraw into anything that seems to promise possibility, even if it is possibility in the most negative sense:

- We have affairs,
- We party excessively,
- We risk our jobs by neglecting work,
- We pour our money into risky investments,
- We gamble.

These false replacements are destructive and hurt us, but as long as they can create a feeling of possibility, we use them to feel better.

Conclusion

These four needs are essential because they create the necessary environment for our minds to function. If one of our essential needs goes completely unsatisfied, our ego is unable to make a good decision – an unthinkable thought that questions the ego's very existence. Left without a constructive option, our ego shuts us down until it has resolved the situation. Often, the ego will invent a false replacement to keep functioning. If our ego fails to resolve the situation on its own, we need help from outside.

Contribution and growth: our non-essential needs

Our needs for contribution and growth are different from our needs for certainty, possibility, love/connection, and significance. Contribution defines our need to help others, to contribute to society, and help our species survive. Growth defines our need to develop our abilities, to grow mentally, and to learn and discover new things.

- Our non-essential needs develop later in life because they spring mostly from the super-ego. Even little kids want to feel certainty, possibility, love/connection, and significance, but they are mostly indifferent about contribution and growth – their super-egos are still developing. As we get older, our super-egos become more important, and we start to feel the needs for contribution and growth.

- Our non-essential needs are long-term oriented. Our ego understands that contribution and growth are long-term processes and that it is impossible to grow and contribute every day. Therefore, we can go decades without satisfying these needs.

- Our non-essential needs are the long-term indicators for the ego's success at making decisions. For the ego, the ultimate measure of success is how much we contribute to our social group. Growth helps us to expand our role and to contribute more. When we are 20, our ego measures its success mostly by using our four essential needs. When we are 40, however, our non-essential needs are more important. Now our ego measures its success largely by how much we have contributed and grown.

- Because they are long-term oriented, our non-essential needs are weaker than our essential needs at any given moment, which makes them negligible. In the long run, however, they are just as important for our happiness as our essential needs.

These differences make sense when we understand why our non-essential needs developed. Throughout evolution, the probability to survive and reproduce depended on how well the other members of our group accepted us. Contribution was essential for gaining acceptance – when we gathered food, fought off predators, or raised children, others recognized us as valuable members of the group and rewarded us with their support. Our need for contribution helped us fit in and increased our chances to reproduce. Similarly, our need for growth motivated us to learn new skills and understand others better, both tools that made us more valuable members of the group. In the long run, growth and contribution were just as valuable to our survival as our essential needs. Certainty, possibility, love/connection, and significance helped us make good decisions on a daily basis, contribution and growth made us become valued members of our social community.

As a result of these evolutionary influences, the needs for contribution and growth still influence our lives today. They are the reason studies show that happy people follow long-term goals – long term goals help us to contribute to something and to grow.

How can we satisfy all our needs?

"The rewards success provides do not nourish the self."
ALEXANDER LOWEN

To be happy, we have to satisfy our essential and nonessential needs. We need to do what has intrinsic value to us on a daily basis while also following long-term goals that help us meet our needs for contribution and growth. When we live our true selves, our essential needs automatically steer us to the fulfillment of our non-essential needs. For example, those of us who follow our true selves when choosing a job will work at something we love and are passionate about, automatically contributing to what's important to us. This passion helps us stay focused and work hard which inevitably leads to growth. At the same time, following long-term goals that can satisfy our non-essential needs adds intrinsic value to our daily lives. The relationship between essential and nonessential needs works both ways. If we live our true selves on a daily basis, we automatically pursue long-term goals. If we pursue long-term goals, we are happy on a daily basis – a powerful connection that makes living our true selves rewarding and essentially important for a good life.

When we neglect our true selves, when we allow fear, insecurity, and the need for approval to trick us into taking a job we feel dispassionate about, we fail to contribute to what's important to us. Since our essential needs require immediate feedback, they can be easily tricked – we can always invent a false replacement. When we want to feel love but are scared to enter a relationship, we can simply get a cat or a dog. This might not be the kind of love we want, but it is a feeling of love none the less. For our essential needs, this makes no difference. Tricking our non-essential needs, however, is impossible. They insist on being satisfied in a certain way – what way depends on our personality. For most of us, a part of contribution means starting a family and caring for our partner and the kids we love. We can find a false replacement for love by getting a cat, but it is impossible to find a false replacement for contribution. Buying a new litter box isn't the same as teaching our kids how to ride a bike.

Because our non-essential needs are long-term indicators can only be understood in hindsight over many years, it is impossible to invent a false replacement when looking back. We either have contributed to our true selves' passions, or we haven't. We either have grown in a way that helps us live our true selves, or we haven't.

This certainty creates most midlife crises. When we are 30, 40, or 50 and look back at what we have done, we often find that we felt somewhat happy most of the time but there's still something big missing. We have ignored our true selves and tricked our essential needs with false replacements which helped us to get by. These false replacements, however, were incapable of directing us to the fulfillment of our non-essential needs, and now we are old enough to feel the effect of our long-term indicators. The ego starts to understand that, by now, we should feel contribution and growth. We had enough time; young age is no longer a valid excuse. The ego starts to question whether what it has done so far has worked and does what it always does when it questions its ability to make good decisions: it shuts us down.

- Our professional careers seems pointless.
- We are no longer sure that our partners are what we want.
- We no longer feel joy from all the things we have bought.
- We lose interest in our friends, hobbies, and families because we start to realize that they are unable to solve our problems.

After a while, the ego must resolve the problem somehow. Since it is incapable of finding a false replacement for our non-essential needs, there are only two options: it can try to suppress these feelings with alcohol, drugs, excessive work, possessions, etc., or it can try to legitimately solve the problem. Obviously, trying to solve the problem would be the better choice, but it is also the harder choice for two reasons:

- Most of us fail to understand the problem. We know that we somehow feel bad, but we lack the necessary knowledge of our own mind's processes to understand why.
- When we understand what's going on, making the necessary changes requires a lot of strength and courage. We may need to change careers, find new friends, or even get a divorce. Most of us are very reluctant to make such big changes.

Strangely enough, these two reasons make it easier for us to create another false replacement and ignore the problem instead of solving it:

- When we want to start a loving family but fight our insecurity with meaningless affairs, we will realize someday that something is missing. We panic and may rush into things – we choose the first person to come along, have kids and start a family that is doomed to fail, which is a false replacement, too.
- When we put our dreams on hold because our social environment disapproves of them, we eventually realize that we might never get to fulfill them. Left without an opportunity to feel growth and contribution, we either become depressed or try to fill the emptiness with false replacements.
- When we fight a lack of significance by overemphasizing our physical attributes and beauty, we eventually realize that we've only generated hollow admiration. Without a true connection with somebody, we are in great danger of filling the void with false replacements.

We can avoid all these problems by living our true selves.

Self-Help Deception #18: To be happy in the long run, we must be willing to neglect our short-term needs.

Conclusion

1. Our behavior is driven by four essential needs (certainty, possibility, love/connection, and significance) and two non-essential needs (contribution and growth). To be truly happy, we have to satisfy all six needs.
2. On a daily basis, our essential needs are stronger than our non-essential needs and can overrule them. This can cause us to ignore our non-essential needs which will lead to problems.
3. Living our true selves will automatically direct us to a life that satisfies all our needs. If we satisfy our essential needs with false replacements, however, we might trick them, but we fail to meet our non-essential needs. Sooner or later, this will result in a deep existential crisis.

Further reading

Martin E. P. Seligman & Steven P. Maier: Failure to Escape Traumatic Shock, Journal of Experimental Psychology, 74, 1-9.

In a classic study that changed psychology, Seligman and Maier concluded that depression is a form of *learned helplessness*. When we believe that it is impossible to create the outcome we desire, we become depressed. A good read for anyone who wants to understand why our egos have needs.

David M. Buss: Evolutionary Psychology.

Buss gives an easy to understand overview of how evolution shaped our minds and what we can learn from these processes. A good read for anyone who wants to learn more about how evolutionary factors still control our behavior.

Chapter 8

How to live our true selves despite our limitations

"You have to lose your illusions while at the same holding on to some sense of possibility. Most importantly your illusions of adult life, of a life without limitations, which I think everyone dreams of at some point. How do you deal with those limitations and move on to a creative life, a spiritual life, a satisfying life, where you can make it through the day and sleep at night?"
BRUCE SPRINGSTEEN

In 1974, Bruce Springsteen released his third record, Born to Run, an anthem to endless possibilities, a life without limitations, and the promise of tomorrow. Three years later, Springsteen's next album, Darkness on the Edge of Town, painted a different picture. Springsteen sang about admitting to limitations, about coming to terms with a life of compromise, and about how to avoid losing ourselves after our dreams have been taken away from us.

At some point in our lives, we all go through a similar transformation. We begin to realize that the dreams of endless possibilities that fueled our youthful spirits might not be the life that awaits us, that there are certain insurmountable limitations, and that these limitations will stop us from fulfilling our dreams. When we are faced with limitations, we have three options:

- We can try to ignore them.
- We can give up on our identity and become who someone else wants us to be.
- We can resolve the conflict constructively.

Currently, most of us choose one of the first two options. Self-help's intrigue largely rests on the implied promise that it can disable our limitations, that these limitations are self-made restrictions of people who fail to understand the secrets of life. Others give up on their dreams, preferring a life in safety, far away from anything that could remind them of the dreams they surrendered. Both options are destructive and suppress a part of who we are. This chapter will show how we can deal with our limitations constructively, and how we can find our true selves after we have given up on everything that we thought we were.

Some philosophers suggest that we go through a transformation, abandoning the life we had designed for ourselves every seven years. But what happens to these abandoned dreams? How can we abandon a dream and still reap the rewards we hoped to get from it? How do we avoid losing ourselves if we constantly change who we are? And do we have only one true self or are there many versions, one for every life period?

Self-help implies that we all have the same true self – the rich, successful, and respected person living in a big white house on the hill. As we have seen, however, happiness is strongly connected to doing what has intrinsic value to us. Since we all find different things intrinsically rewarding, we all have a different true self. Let's get clear on who our true self is, why this concept is so important to achieving happiness, and how we can find and live our true selves.

How can we find our true self?

Determining a few of our false replacements is relatively easy. As soon as we understand the concept of false replacements, most of us can quickly identify one or two of our activities and thought processes as false replacements. Over time, as we use our new knowledge to analyze why we do what we do, we will find more and more false replacements. With every false replacement, we subtract a part of who we thought we were. When we no longer define ourselves by the success we have and how beautiful and how smart we are, when we can feel self-worth without artificial tools such as alcohol, cigarettes, or expensive clothes, all that is left is to be ourselves. This thought can be the starting point for our journey to happiness – but it is also deeply terrifying. For most of us, our true self has been buried under layers of false replacements for years. We have been told what we needed to do and that it was impossible to do what we really wanted to do, maybe even that suffering and self-neglect are essential ingredients of a good life. To be who we ought to be, we have long ago given up asking who we want to be. If we have ever had a connection to our true selves, it was when we were small children, much longer ago than we can remember. Aside from a lack of knowledge, these layers of false replacements are the reason some people question whether they have a true self at all.

The most difficult part about shedding our protective layer of false replacements is finding the reason we created them – the part of our true self we gave up. Most of our mental process is subconscious. We are incapable of fully describing why we love someone or something, why some things make us happy, and why some things make us unhappy. Even if we spend years trying to rationalize our thinking, no explanation will ever be sufficient. Understanding why we created a false replacement and uncovering the true self behind it requires that we shed light on this subconscious process. Let's start by finding out where our true selves come from.

How to find our true self by following our passions

Living our true self means doing what suits our character, doing what has intrinsic value to us, and it means not to suppress any part of who we are and to avoid extrinsic activities as much as possible:

- For someone with high activity levels, living their true self might mean to take a job that requires physical activity even if they could make more money working in an office.
- For someone who is compassionate and loving, living their true self might mean to take a job with a social component even if their parents urge them to become a corporate lawyer.
- For someone who enjoys being alone, living their true self might mean to remain single even if getting married is the socially accepted norm.
- For someone who sees no value in driving an expensive car, living their true self might mean to drive a used cheaper make even if they could easily afford a BMW that would help them gain social status.
- For someone who loves math but dislikes languages, living their true self might mean choosing a career related to math and physics even if there are currently better employment opportunities in other fields.

Some people see more beauty when they look at the stars than anywhere here on earth. They are unable to explain why they are drawn to pictures from distant galaxies, they simply are. Science can't fully explain these predispositions, but we know from chapter 3 ("Can we become anything we want?") that they exist and shape our lives. Neil deGrasse Tyson, the most famous astrophysicist of our time, often told the story of the time when he first left the Bronx and saw the stars in a sky with no light pollution. He immediately knew that this was what he wanted to do. The stars fascinated him like nothing he had seen before, even though he was incapable of explaining why.

Other people find the same beauty when they look at wildlife here on earth. Leonardo da Vinci and Charles Darwin were both drawn to nature from a young age. Both spent hours every day drawing animals. Darwin discovered evolution; da Vinci was the first to draw realistic pictures of animals and people, among other things. Darwin and da Vinci chose different life paths, but they both made a decision that is crucial to living our true selves: they did what had intrinsic value to them in their professional lives. They followed their passion, the path their genetic makeup had laid out for them. Because Darwin and da Vinci were both passionate about nature and about understanding how our world works, they created careers that helped them live these passions. Their passion gave their work intrinsic value.

Equipped with an intrinsically rewarding career that made false replacements unnecessary, they put more effort into their work than anybody else and mastered their fields in a way nobody had done before them. Darwin, who had never been in contact with sailors before and was uneasy with their rough customs, agreed to a 5-year voyage on the HMS Beagle to study nature. Even though he spent most of his time seasick and alone in a small cabin with no amenities, Darwin persevered. His passion made the voyage intrinsically rewarding in spite of the hardship and the unfamiliar environment. Without this passion, Darwin would never have made the discoveries that eventually led him to create his theory of evolution. Similarly, Leonardo da Vinci had to overcome obstacles that would have stopped less passionate colleagues. He was an illegitimate son, and his only chance to be an artist depended on finding a rich patron to draw for. Being frightened that such a dependent work relationship might rob him of the freedom to pursue his passion, Leonardo did something that was unheard of in his time: he became the world's first entrepreneurial artist and inventor. Without an abundant passion for his work, da Vinci would never have taken this risk – and would never have changed the world the way he did.

In his book *Mastery*, Robert Greene analyzes the life paths of masters such as da Vinci and Darwin – masters from all fields and periods of time. Greene concludes that all the masters he analyzed followed similar life paths – paths that are fundamentally different from the ones self-help books want us to follow. They chose a career that was intrinsically rewarding to them and used their passion to reach a skill level nobody had ever reached before. Unfortunately, Greene succumbs to the generalization that following the same path as these masters will make us all achieve mastery, too. That is not true. Da Vinci and Darwin were each unique minds in unique situations, and many things had to fall into place for them to become who they became. For most of us, our ceiling is considerably lower. Nonetheless, choosing an intrinsically rewarding career path will get us as close to our ceiling as possible.

Taking a similar approach as Greene, Malcolm Gladwell analyzed success stories for his book *Outliers*. Gladwell concluded that the people behind all great success stories spent roughly 10,000 hours perfecting their craft. These 10,000 hours gave them the necessary skill to do what others failed to do. While Gladwell's reasoning is perfectly sound, he ignores the two most important questions his theory creates:

1. How can we motivate ourselves to put 10,000 hours into something? How can we work multiple hours every day, studying, practicing, and learning, without any guarantee of success and no initial positive reinforcement? How can we possibly fight off disenchantment after we have put in the first 1,000 hours, realizing that we are still relatively unskilled and far from where we want to go?
2. Are we equally likely to achieve success in any field by putting 10,000 hours into it? Or can we only achieve success in certain fields, having to make more effort in some, less in others, while success will always elude us in certain fields, regardless of the effort we put in?

The answer to these questions is in our genetic makeup. An inherent passion can turn the diligent, years-long process of devoting 10,000 hours to a field into an intrinsically rewarding adventure we gladly undertake – regardless of initial success. Similarly, a genetic predisposition for a certain field makes success more easily achievable. Depending on our genetic suitability, it might take us 9,500 hours to achieve mastery in one field and 11,000 in another, while we can never become masters in some fields

Choosing an intrinsically rewarding career path can do two things for us:

1. It will help us make the most of our abilities. We might not all change the world, but when we love what we do, we put in the necessary effort to make the most of our abilities.
2. It will help us be happy. We spend such a large part of our time either at work, thinking about work, or preparing for work that we need this time to have intrinsic value to us, or we will inevitably start to experience the awful consequences we discussed in previous chapters.

This concept applies to all aspects of our lives: relationships, hobbies, shopping, etc. Focusing on activities that have intrinsic value to us helps us make the most of our abilities and achieve happiness:

- Friendships we enjoy provide us with more happiness and will be more reliable than friendships we form for convenience, our own benefit, or other extrinsic reasons.
- A partner we love and enjoy spending time with provides us with more happiness and a more durable relationship than a partner we chose because they are pretty, rich, or can impress others, or because we think that we are incapable of finding someone else or that we deserve to be unhappy.
- Buying a car that helps us do what has intrinsic value to us – travel, drive our kids, get to work – provides us with more happiness than getting into debt for an excessively expensive car to gain status.
- Buying functional, timeless, and reasonably priced clothes that are a good fit for what we want to do provides us with more joy than investing large amounts of money in buying designer clothes, in chasing every new trend, or in collecting more clothes than we can wear. Think Steve Jobs and Elon Musk instead of Kim Kardashian or Paris Hilton.

Are there multiple versions of the true self?

Leonardo da Vinci and Charles Darwin followed similar passions but took different paths. The same passion for nature helped one to become an artist, an inventor, and an engineer, and the other to become a geologist and a natural historian. Very likely, each of them would have found the other's career highly interesting, but equally likely neither of them would have achieved the same level of success at the other's path, even though it was connected to the same passion. This is interesting. Apparently, following passion is not the only requirement for achieving success and happiness. There must be a second factor. What?

As we have seen before, our genes shape our identity. What we are drawn to and what we are good at is at least partially a result of our genetic makeup. Da Vinci and Darwin had their unique genetic strengths and weaknesses, too. Had they tried to live their passion by creating a career based on their weaknesses, they would have spent their lives fighting an uphill battle, which would never have resulted in the level of success that cultivating their talents allowed them to have.

Charles Darwin and Leonardo da Vinci had different talents, which is why they followed the same passion in different directions. For both, however, the secret of success was to use their talents to live their passion. A similar approach can help us find success and happiness, too. Our passions predetermine which general direction we should go in, our strengths carve out our specific path. Simply doing what has intrinsic value is insufficient to guarantee success. We have to do what has intrinsic value to us in a way that suits our strengths.

Combining our strengths and passions creates our true self – the undistorted combination of what we want to do *and* what we can do.

What we are truly passionate about

While self-help also advises us to follow our passion, it makes the mistake of tying this passion to a career. This misconception has led many of us to think back on our lives and on the things we enjoyed, and, as we find an activity that made us happy, to conclude that we must be passionate about this activity – which is a mistake. For example, most of us have happy childhood memories of doing something that came naturally to us. For me, it was always writing. I started simple websites and blogs and wrote about what was important to me, even though nobody wanted to read it. From these memories, it would be compelling but wrong to conclude that I was passionate about writing. Many aspiring authors make the mistake of studying journalism and taking a job at a newspaper, where they write about what someone else tells them to. Often, these authors end up hating their jobs. Why? When these authors were young, they did more than simply write. Just like me, they wrote about what they loved. This passion fueled their writing. I wrote about psychology and philosophy because I wanted to understand myself and the world better and I figured that there must be other people who were interested in the same things. That was my true passion. Writing was just a tool. Any tool to help me live my passion would have been an equally good fit for a career. For example, I love music that helps people lead better lives and American football, which I consider being the best character-building game in the world – both are tools that helped me understand myself and the world better. If I had the necessary skills, I could just as easily be happy as an athlete or a musician – both jobs would enable me to contribute to the values I'm passionate about. Unfortunately, I lack these skills, and these careers are impossible for me.

As long as different careers help us live the same values, each of them can make us happy. If we misinterpret passion as being tied to a certain career, we can set ourselves up for bitter disappointment. For me, writing has become a tool to live my passion. If I had become an author writing poor fiction or unimportant local stories for a newspaper, I would have been depressed within days. The intrinsic value of writing this book came from the topic I wrote about, not from writing in itself.

Self-Help Deception #19: We can be passionate about a specific career.

It's never a certain activity we are passionate about. It is always the values that this activity helps us contribute to. When different activities help us contribute to the same values, we can be equally happy doing any of them. To make our lives easier and to enjoy some success at what we do, we should choose the activity for which we are the most talented. Using our strengths to live the values we are passionate about helps us make the most of every aspect of our lives:

- A hobby that helps us contribute to the values we are passionate about will only be intrinsically rewarding if we are any good at it. If nobody wants us on their team, if we never get in a game, or if we lack the skills to complete what we want to do, our hobby will be a disappointment.
- Buying what helps us live our true selves makes us happy and helps us treat these things better than things we buy to keep up with the Joneses.
- For some of us, starting a family and raising children is the most important thing in the world. If our partner can provide for the entire family, it might make sense for those of us to be stay-at-home dads or moms. As long as this is the best way to contribute to what we care about, we must avoid allowing insecurities and outside pressure to trick us into a life that makes us unhappy.

If we can't work in the jobs we were originally passionate about; we can find other jobs that help us contribute to the same values but better suit our strengths. The same applies to relationships, hobbies, and any other aspect of life. As long as we contribute to the values we are passionate about, any life can make us happy. For each of us, there is a large variety of life paths that our true selves allow. If one path gets taken away, we can find another way to contribute to the same values. This explains why humans deal so well with adversity. We can always find another relationship, another job, or another hobby that helps us contribute to the same values and be equally happy.

The secret of happiness is contribution

Living the values we are passionate about is a well-sounding but vague recommendation. To make our knowledge applicable, we have to determine what it means to live certain values. As research by Sonja Lyubomirsky indicates, living the values we are passionate about means to contribute to them.

In one experiment, researchers of the University of British Columbia gave students \$5 or \$20. They told half of these students to spend the money on themselves, paying a bill, paying off debt, or buying something. The other half of the students were told to buy something for someone else or to donate the money. The researchers then measured how much happier both groups of students became. Those students who had spent the money on others reported to be significantly happier than the students who had spent the money on themselves. The amount of money made no difference. What mattered was on whom the money was spent.

In two similar studies, the same researchers first compared more than 600 Americans on how they spend their money and how happy they are. How much money people spent on themselves had no influence on their happiness, but the more people spent on others and donated to charity, the happier these people became. Then the researchers focused on employees who had received a bonus of \$5,000 from their company. Again, those employees who spent the bonus on themselves showed no increase in happiness, but those employees who spent the bonus on others or donated it to charity became significantly happier.

In her book *The Myths of Happiness*, Sonja Lyubomirsky explains these findings:

- When we give to others, we feel better about ourselves. We contribute, we feel love/connection and significance.
- We feel better about the people or the values to which we contribute. Knowing that there are good things worth contributing to helps us enjoy ourselves and the world around us more.
- Knowing that we are doing something to make the world a better place helps us feel less distracted about the world's suffering. Things might not be perfect, but at least, we are doing something about it.
- We are less distracted by our little problems. When we try to end world hunger, to educate the youth, or to travel to Mars, a noisy neighbor becomes a minor inconvenience.
- We appreciate our good fortune more because we see how much we can contribute and that others have much less.

- We create new friendships with the people who are contributing to the same causes we believe in.

These results are significant. They show that the values our true selves want to contribute to must be focused outwardly, not inwardly. Self-help implies that we can be passionate about things such as being rich and famous and that we can pursue our true selves by trying to become stars. Being famous and similar inwardly focused goals in themselves have no intrinsic value, we pursue them because we want to achieve something else and because we have fallen for the misconception that we will be happy if a certain event occurs. These goals are false replacements - it is impossible to contribute to wealth or fame. Only the things we can contribute to can be values, things that help someone else or humanity as a whole. Being famous can only be a tool to contribute to our values, for example by bringing attention to an issue or raising money.

Values we can contribute to can be:

- Advancing a scientific frontier (as engineers, scientists, test subjects, donors, astronauts, professors, assistants, facility managers at a university, politicians that increase scientific funding, teachers, etc.),
- Helping raise children (as teachers, housewives, volunteers, social workers, sports coaches, donors, etc.),
- Making our city more beautiful (as politicians, social workers, volunteers, architects, house owners, garden decorators, designers, etc.),
- Building something that helps people lead better lives (as engineers, factory workers, designers, managers, office employees, etc.),
- Helping people stay in contact with their loved ones (as mailmen, technicians, engineers, designers, etc.),
- Helping people have a good retirement (as social workers, investment managers, doctors, volunteers, friends, children, etc.),
- Helping people enjoy their favorite sport (as players, coaches, stadium workers, ground keepers, front office employees, public transport employees, etc.),
- Curing diseases (as doctors, scientists, engineers, social workers, volunteers, etc.),
- And many more.

Activities that contribute nothing to values we are passionate about are *always* false replacements. These include the following examples:

- Heavy drinking,
- Doing drugs,
- Smoking,

- Excessive partying
- Excessive shopping,
- Endless TV-watching,
- Meaningless sex,
- Working in jobs we hate,
- Having social connections we do not enjoy,
- Being in a loveless relationship,
- Youth slang or anything else that emphasizes style over content,
- Buying expensive clothes, cars, or other things that have no additional value other than a brand name we can use to deal with our insecurities.

While such destructive activities as doing drugs are always false replacements, activities such as watching TV or having a beer with friends might serve our true selves when done in moderation. They can help us to relax and to recharge our self-control batteries (see Chapter 11, "How can we show more self-control?"). These activities only become a problem when they become an end in themselves. When having a beer with friends turns into finding someone to drink with, when watching a show we like turns into finding something to watch, and when celebrating a success or birthday turns into finding a reason to party, we have skewed the activity's inherent meaning. We no longer do it because we want to, but because we want to achieve something else with it. It has become extrinsic, and it will leave a void inside us.

Sometimes we make the mistake of thinking that doing what has intrinsic value to us means committing to our weaker selves – to party our lives away or to spend the entire day on the couch watching TV. That is not true. Being a drunk or a couch potato can hardly contribute to any values. These activities are false replacements, ways to retreat from a life that makes us unhappy, and the exact opposite of our true selves. Doing what has intrinsic value to us always means to add value to something – anything that is as inwardly focused as watching TV or playing video games can never be the main part of our true selves. While we need recreation, it is always a means to an end; it is never an end in itself.

Self-Help Deception #20: All our dreams are equal. They can make us equally happy and have equal reasons to be pursued. (The truth: Dreams can be the result of a true self or a false replacement. We need to distinguish one from the other. Dreams that are false replacements will not make us happy.)

With this simple definition, we have demystified the true self. Self-help does very little to explain conclusively who we are. Depending on the expert, we can be anything from a mindless machine made for hard work to a master of the universe that can influence quantum physics. All of these concepts are nonsense. We are the combination of what we can do and what we like to do, and that is it. When we use our strengths to live our passions, we make the most of our abilities, we benefit society the most, and we live the best lives possible.

How to develop our personality

Laura King, an American professor at the University of Missouri, Columbia, studies how we deal with unfulfilled dreams. If we dream of becoming an astronaut but have to realize that this dream will never come true, what do we do? While regrets are a common aspect of life – in one survey, 90 percent of all subjects admitted deep regrets – people deal with regrets very differently. King analyzes these different ways and the results they generate, allowing for conclusions about which ways work better than others. The way advertised in self-help books is the worst way of all.

As King found, the best way to deal with regrets is to face them head on. We can free ourselves from the burden of broken dreams by understanding them as learning opportunities, as something that we can analyze and use to create a better future. Those people who have analyzed why they had a dream, what they can learn from it, and how they can integrate these lessons into the new version of themselves were significantly happier than those people who either suppressed self-analysis and acted as if their dream had never existed or held on to unachievable goals. The self-analysis process King talks about is the process we laid out so far. When a dream falls apart, as many dreams inevitably do, we can analyze what drew us to this dream.

- Did we use it as a false replacement for a part of our true selves that we suppressed? If so, we can become happier by living this part of our true selves in its original way.
- Were we drawn to this dream because it would have helped us to contribute to the values we are passionate about? If so, we can find other ways to contribute to the same values.

Either way, we can create better lives. We can understand our own complexity, develop our personality, and shape ourselves into more mature adults.

Many of us avoid this essential self-analysis process because it can be painful. We have to face the possibility that we pursued an unachievable goal, that we were wrong to have aspirations, or, worst of all, that we easily could have succeeded but failed due to our shortcomings. One of the reasons people read self-help books is to keep their dreams alive, to find a way to hold on to what seems hopeless by any reasonable evaluation. With this empty promise, self-help books prevent us from healthy self-reflection. They tell us never to give up on a dream, to keep pushing on without any doubts – the exact opposite of personal development. As King's research shows, the worst thing we can do is to ignore our regrets. When we act as if our dreams had never existed, we learn nothing. We invested a lot of time, effort, and heart into something that generated no returns, which makes us feel ashamed of having the dream in the first place. To cope with this shame, we generate false replacements and make our lives worse. When we analyze our broken dreams, we can learn from them and grow. While this process is initially painful, our new-found knowledge helps us pursue new dreams that have intrinsic value to us, and that can generate the same rewards as our original dream, integrating our broken dreams into better versions of ourselves. We can now find ways to contribute to the values we are passionate about, ways that would have been impossible without our broken dreams. We add intrinsic value to our broken dreams, even if they are something as sad as an illness. We no longer need to feel ashamed for not realizing our dreams; we can move on to what lies ahead. This is why many cancer survivors help to spread awareness about the disease – it gives their suffering intrinsic meaning, it helps them develop a new, stronger version of themselves, and it helps them contribute to the values they are passionate about.

Self-Help Deception #21: When we encounter difficulties, we should not diverge from our way, and should not allow a dream to fall apart. (The truth: To be happy, we need to grow. Broken dreams are important learning opportunities that we must not waste, opportunities that can help us to re-emerge as stronger, better, and wiser versions of ourselves.)

Conclusion

1. Consciously combining skill and passion is the key to happiness *and* to making the most of any aspect of our lives. Our true selves are where passion and skill unite.
2. Passion turns otherwise unrewarding tasks into intrinsically rewarding activities, enabling us to invest more time and effort into them. Over time, this effort helps us develop our skills faster and to a higher level than we could in any other field – by living our true selves, we create a competitive edge in any field of life.
3. When one version of our true selves is taken away from us, we can find other ways to contribute to the values we are passionate about. This process helps us understand ourselves better and develop complex personalities – essential requirements for a good, happy life.

Further reading

Laura A. King & Joshua A. Hicks: Whatever happened to "What might have been"? Regrets, happiness, and maturity, American Psychologist 62, 2007, 625-636.

Laura King's insightful article on how to deal with broken dreams and abandoned selves.

Aknin, L., et al.: Prosocial spending and well-being: Cross-cultural evidence for a psychological universal.
The aforementioned experiment where students had to spend money on themselves or others and were measured on how happy their spending made them.

Dunn, E.W., Aknin, L.B., & Norton, M.I.: Spending money on others promotes happiness, Science 319, 1967-88.
The aforementioned study on spending habits of Americans, concluding that spending more money on others makes us happier.

Chapter 9

How to stop doing what hurts us

"Too many people buy things they do not need with money they do not have to impress people they do not know."

ROBERT KIYOSAKI

Two years ago I was planning to open a bar in Munich. One day, I was talking to my business coach, by all common measures a successful man. He owned his own business and was invested in a few others, he drove a shiny new car, lived in a big house, and had a beautiful wife. I was trying to create the life my coach was living. Even though opening my own bar would have put me into a lot of debt and tied me to one place for at least the next ten years, I was willing to accept that. When we were talking, however, my coach casually said something that changed my life. We were discussing the plan to get the bar set up and ready for opening when he asked me how I was planning to pay for my expenses until the bar would turn a profit. I told him that I had all my essential expenses covered with passive income and work I could do online – a confession that I felt bad about. My humble earnings were far from what my coach was making. While he was coasting around in a brand new top of the line Audi SUV, I was barely keeping my 20-year-old Chrysler van alive. I felt inferior. Still, my coach, the rich and successful guy, the man I was aspiring to become like, quietly said, "Well, I guess then you are living the dream. I have to work two weeks each month just to pay for that stupid car." As you can probably imagine, after this conversation, I never opened the bar. I spent weeks wondering about why my coach was unable to cancel the lease on his car. He obviously would have enjoyed working less, and he knew that he only owned the car to appear successful, but he still was unable to free himself from it. What made him hang on to what he knew was bad for him? And how can we avoid making the same mistake in our lives? Self-help, with its inherent focus on adding more to our lives to achieve happiness, never tackles these questions.

To do a better job, we will follow a three-step process. We will find a way to identify our false replacements; we will point out the reasons why eliminating false replacements is difficult, and we will find a way to make the process easier.

Step 1: How can we identify our false replacements?

To uncover our true selves, we have to discover and eliminate our false replacements. This is not easy. Without the necessary knowledge, it can be a nearly impossible challenge to make sense of the complex mix of feelings, desires, and urges we experience every day. Questioning this direction is essential to understanding whether we do something as a true self or as a false replacement, but if we challenge our actions with the wrong questions, we can never get the right answers.

We can identify our false replacements by questioning the motives behind our actions, by asking ourselves, "Why am I doing this?" There are four possible answers to this question:

1. We do something because we want to do it from a deep inner part of ourselves.
2. We do something because we think we have to, but we have no inner desire to do it and see no greater sense in it.
3. We do something because we want to do it, but we know that it will hurt us mentally, physically, financially, or in some other way.
4. We do something because it aids a bigger plan we want to carry out from a deep inner part of ourselves.

Possibility 1 is the ideal.

We do what is intrinsically rewarding to us and meets our needs. Our ego has brought our id and our super-ego in alignment. If there was a conflict between the subconscious parts of our mind, the ego has resolved it constructively. Ideally, this is what happens when our partners ask us to help them with something. Our id enjoys helping those we love, our super-ego understands that mutual help is important in any relationship. Our ego can easily compromise these two points and make a decision that satisfies every aspect of our psyche.

Unfortunately, such easy decisions rarely happen in real life. Most of our decisions are far more complex – we have contradicting motivations, we want more than one outcome from a situation, and we might have conflicting goals. When our partners want us to help them, the id might be lazy, and the super-ego might be scared that someone takes advantage of us. This would make the decision more difficult. We want to help, but we also want to stay on the couch, and we want to avoid appearing weak. Most decisions offer at least this kind of complexity.

Possibility 2 is a destructive solution.

We do something because we think we have to but feel no desire to do it. In this situation, the ego has allowed the super-ego to overrule and suppress the id – a destructive way to resolve our inner conflict. To find another outlet for the id's desires, the ego will sooner or later create a false replacement. We are left with two activities – the original activity and the false replacement – but neither can satisfy our needs. We will keep creating false replacements and start the vicious cycle. For many of us, this situation happens when we try to find a job. We start out with idealistic hopes and goals, but fear, insecurity and the need for approval trick us into taking a job we think is safe, but that has no intrinsic value to us and fails to make us happy.

Possibility 3 is a false replacement.

Possibility 3 is the exact opposite of possibility 2. We do something because we want to, but have to suppress our conscience to do it. The ego has allowed the id to overrule the super-ego. This is what happens when we spend more than we want on shopping, eat more than we need, or drink more than we know is healthy for us. This behavior always points to a false replacement. We have suppressed a part of our true selves and are now experiencing the false replacement we created as a defense mechanism against this desire. Since this false replacement fails to make us happy, too, we have to create another one, and then another one. The only way out of this vicious cycle is to find the part of our true selves we suppressed which made us create the first false replacement. When we start to integrate this part of our true selves back into our lives, we eliminate the need for all false replacements we created because of it.

For many people, their entire lives consist of possibilities 2 and 3. They make destructive decisions and then create false replacements to deal with them.

Possibility 4 is a constructive solution.

Our super-ego was in conflict with our id, but the ego found a way to align both. This situation occurs when we deal with life's challenges in a constructive way. We will rarely find such perfect situations as in possibility 1. In real life, we will mostly encounter possibilities 2 and 3 – both signs of false replacements. Let's see how we can transform these destructive solutions into a constructive solution, as in possibility 4.

Step 2: Why do we hang on to false replacements?

Discovering a false replacement is much easier than eliminating it. After all, there is a reason we created it in the first place, something that made us neglect a part of who we are. Now, we try to do what we were incapable of doing in the past. To understand why this is so difficult, let's go back to the example of the football player who risked his life by trying to play through a spleen injury but avoided all risks off the field. This football player often talked about how much he hated his job, how he felt bored and imprisoned. But he also talked about how much he needed the money. Obviously, his id and his super-ego were in conflict. His id urged him to find a more active job; his super-ego told him to take the money. Since he resolved this conflict unconstructively – his ego suppressed the id and did what the super-ego demanded – he needed to find an outlet for the suppressed part of the id. This outlet was taking insane risks while playing football. When I joined the team, this player was already in his mid-30s. Every season, he announced that this would be his last year, only to eventually realize that, without having eliminated the need for his false replacement, he was incapable of giving it up. Now, five years later, he is still playing.

To eliminate the source of his false replacement, this football player would have needed to change his entire life. He would have had to leave the job he hated and find a new career. He would have had to explain this decision to his wife and his child, his friends, family, and co-workers, admitting to everyone that he had lied to himself for years, that the tough guy act was only a facade, and that he was just scared to do what he truly wanted to do. He would have to publicly renounce his current false self. Then he could live his love for football in a less destructive way, either by only playing when he is healthy or by finally retiring and starting to coach.

A coming out of this scale is redeeming but scary. We fear that our social relationships might get damaged, that our friends will fail to understand why we changed, that people might make fun of us, and, as a consequence, that we will end up alone. We are insecure, and we question whether we are destroying our lives on a whim. These feelings can stop us from doing what we know is right. We overvalue the importance of our false replacements and ignore all other shared qualities of our social relationships, which tricks us into keeping a false self alive for years, simply because we are afraid of what might happen if we give it up.

Self-Help Deception #22: Giving up is a sign of weakness. (The truth: If we give up to let go of a false replacement and dedicate ourselves to what is truly important to us, giving up is a sign of strength.)

Step 3: How can we eliminate false replacements?

As a concept from relationship theory tells us, keeping a false replacement alive is dangerous. One field of relationship theory analyzes why people stay in a relationship after they know that it has failed and has no future – a situation similar to people holding on to a false self. Psychologists have found that we have an inner gauge that tells us whether we get enough out of a relationship or not. This gauge subtracts the perceived costs of a relationship from its perceived advantages. Subconsciously, according to the theory, we then compare the result to the minimum outcome we want to get from a relationship, and to what we expect to get if we leave it. Whether we get what we expect or not determines how happy we are with the relationship, but whether or not we think that we can get more elsewhere determines if we leave. We might be deeply unhappy with a relationship, but as long as we believe that things will get worse if we end them, we stay in the relationship and stay unhappy.

Adapted to false replacements, this theory tells us that simply being unhappy with a false replacement is insufficient for us to give it up – we need to be sure that our lives are worse now than they would be if we abandon the false replacement. This is a big hurdle. We succumb to focalism and overvalue the importance of the false replacement to our social relationships, to our career, and to our life in general. We often expect all hell to break loose if we let a false replacement go. Therefore, our lives have to get dramatically bad before we voluntarily eliminate a false replacement.

This explains why we keep doing what's bad for us after we know that it is bad for us, why we keep smoking, stay in failed relationships, and keep working in jobs we hate, or why we drink too much – we are still uncertain that our lives would be better if we let our false replacement go. Unfortunately, there is no simple concept to make this process easier. All we can do is understand the dangers of false replacements. When we know that a false replacement will not simply vanish, that it will not stop making us unhappy until we hit rock bottom, we gain the power to eliminate false replacements before they get out of hand:

- By knowing that things will only get worse if we keep a false replacement alive, we lower our perceived well-being.
- By knowing that we should refrain from allowing focalism to trick us into overestimating the importance of a false replacement, we raise our expectancy of what we can get without the false replacement.

Both factors combined make us quit false replacements earlier, when we have a higher quality of life left than if we failed to understand how false replacements work.

How can we make good every-day decisions?

The best way to eliminate false replacements from our lives is not to create them in the first place. Therefore, we now have to adapt our findings to our everyday lives. With almost every decision we make, we face the risk of creating a false replacement. When we choose a career, for example, the id wants to work on something we love and have fun doing. The super-ego, on the other hand, wants us to take a safe job that secures us a steady income and the respect of others for the rest of our lives. Instead of going all-in in one direction, suppressing the other part of our mind, there are plenty of ways in which we can resolve this conflict constructively.

- We could take a part-time job that helps us put a roof over our heads and get some experience while we pursue our passion in our spare time. After a while, we can decide which direction to go in. More than likely, the id will either have found that the secure job is enjoyable after all, or the super-ego will have to admit that our passion might enable us to lead a respectable life, too. Either way, the ego will have an easy decision to make.

- We could set a fixed date or a fixed amount of money we can spend on trying to turn our passion into a living. If it works out, great. If it fails, we can always go back to the safer alternative.

Of course, there are more possibilities. Which one is right for each of us depends on our personality, our life situation, and which other passions we have. The final decision has to be ours, nobody can make it for us. Letting someone else make a decision for us is always a false replacement for a lack of certainty.

We can make good decisions if we understand the different urges inside our minds, why we are drawn in multiple directions simultaneously. When we know that this conflict is not a sign of indecisiveness or weakness but a natural result of the two subconscious elements of our minds and that this conflict helps us to understand both sides of the situation, we can handle the conflict and resolve it constructively by comparing both alternatives and finding a compromise that makes the best of both. This mental process helps us to uncover previously hidden solutions that help us lead better lives.

For example, most of us think that we have only three options when it comes to dealing with nervousness:

1. Never be nervous by nature,
2. Suppress our nervousness, or
3. Allow our nervousness to ruin what we are doing.

Obviously, alternative one would be the ideal. Unfortunately, when we have to give a talk in front of a crowd and get nervous, there's little we can do about it. In a situation like this, most people either try to suppress their nervousness or allow it to take their skills away. When we understand our mental process, we can understand why we are nervous: our super-ego is contemplating what could happen if we screw things up. This might sound simple, but it helps us realize that nervousness is never meant in a harmful way. There's no need to suppress it or to let it ruin what we are doing.

Nervousness is our brain's attempt to tell us that what we are doing is important and that we must do a good job at it. Suppressing this feeling would mean to suppress a part of who we are, giving in to it would suppress another part. Both solutions are destructive and force the creation of false replacements. We can resolve this conflict constructively by integrating our nervousness into what we are doing, not by suppressing it. Again, how we do this depends on our personality. For many of us, nervousness arises when we do something that we know we are not good at. In this case, we can use nervousness as an indicator for what we should practice more or for what we need to learn more about.

When nervousness happens in situations that we are familiar with, we can use it as a support mechanism that helps us be at our best. Bruce Springsteen re-labeled his nervousness before a concert as excitement, thereby giving it a positive spin. Nervousness helps him to be alert and ready when he gets on stage, not tired and bored. This simple trick integrates all his emotions into what he's doing. He can accept his nervousness, not creating a false replacement. Many other rock stars that have suppressed their nervousness started using alcohol or drugs to calm their nerves – they created a false replacement. We see similar lines of dealing with nervousness when men approach women. Some integrate their nervousness constructively by paying close attention to what the woman is saying, some try to numb their nervousness with alcohol. Which side would you rather be on?

Nonetheless, even with this knowledge, we can never eliminate all our false replacements. Nobody has such a perfect inner gauge that he can eliminate every false replacement immediately when he recognizes it. Fighting against false replacements is an ongoing process, a life-long effort that requires us to pay constant attention to our thoughts and motives – but it is well worth the effort.

Self-Help Deception #23: Compromise is a sign of weakness.

Conclusion

1. We can identify false replacements by searching for activities and thought patterns that we either do not want to do but do them anyway or that we keep doing even though we know they hurt us.
2. Our minds eliminate a false replacement only when it is sure that our lives will be better off without it. Since we fear the unknown, are insecure, and need approval, we overestimate how bad our lives will be without the false replacement and wait until we hit rock bottom before we give up on it.
3. By understanding how false replacements work, we can eliminate them earlier – before they ruin our lives.

Further reading

Joseph Burgo: Why Do I Do That? Psychological Defense Mechanisms and the Hidden Ways They Shape Our Lives.
See Chapter 5 ("Why we do what makes us unhappy").

Part II

Applying our philosophy of life

Chapter 10

How to develop our talents

"Every artist was first an amateur."
RALPH WALDO EMERSON

I have never learned English in my life. While I'm a native German speaker and knew nobody to talk English to for the first 22 years of my life, I completed my first 50-page university paper in English at the age of 20. I learned English by watching American movies, TV series, documentaries and football broadcasts. Later I read English books and studied English song lyrics. English was a necessary skill for doing what I was passionate about, which helped me learn English by accident, without ever focusing on it. It might be true that I have a talent for English or languages in general, but my passion developed my talent into a skill. Similarly, most people who mastered a skill used passion as the motor to develop their talents. This chapter will focus on how we can do the same.

We are all born with certain talents. Some of us are strong, some are smart, some are pretty; some are good with words, some are good with math, and some are good with their hands. We can't influence which talents we are born with – but we can influence how well we develop our talents into skills and how well our talents help us to lead a good life. As we have seen earlier, passion is the driving force that develops our talents into skills. How does this process work? And how can we maximize the returns we get? This chapter will answer these questions.

Many people make the mistake of choosing a job that only focuses on their skills. A multitude of talented writers takes jobs at newspapers where they are assigned to topics they hate. They have the perfect skill set for the job, and they could write great texts, but without the necessary passion, they just put in the minimum effort to not get fired. By the time they are 40, their lack of effort has made them average. Now somebody younger could do the same job for less money.

In his book *Mastery*, Robert Greene analyzes how masters of a field transformed their talents into skills. Greene writes:

"The problem we face is that this form of power and intelligence is either ignored as a subject of study or is surrounded by all kinds of myths and misconceptions, all of which only add to the mystery. We imagine that creativity and brilliance just appear out of nowhere, the fruit of natural talent, or perhaps a good mood, or an alignment of the stars. It would be an immense help to clear up the mystery – to name this feeling of power, to examine its roots, to define the kind of intelligence that leads to it, and to understand how it can be manufactured and maintained."
ROBERT GREENE

With this assessment, Greene outlines precisely the problem this chapter is trying to solve. For his answer, Greene identifies a list of what he calls "masters" of their field, people who were in total control of the matter they were dealing with. He then analyzes how these people reached mastery and tries to find common features. According to Greene, all highly successful people throughout history followed the same path. Greene outlines a three-step process for turning our talents into skills and creating what he calls "mastery" of a field.

1. Apprenticeship

Greene calls the first phase of his process the apprenticeship. In this phase, we are outsiders to our field, trying to learn the basic elements and rules. Since we lack a solid understanding of our field, our potential is limited. We are unaware of what it takes to succeed or where to start learning. Greene lists many masters of their fields and tells the story of their apprenticeships:

- Leonardo da Vinci started working as an apprentice for the artist Verrocchio at age 14, a time in which he both learned theoretical concepts and acquired a vast range of technical skills. Without this apprenticeship, probably the most literal example of an apprenticeship in Greene's book, da Vinci's later accomplishments would have been impossible.

- Charles Darwin sailed around the world on the HMS Beagle for five years, a time in which he laid the foundation for his theory of evolution by natural selection. Without the boundless variety of species Darwin encountered during this trip, his world-changing discovery would have been impossible.

- From age 12 to 17, Benjamin Franklin worked as an apprentice in his brother's printing shop. He read endlessly, educated himself, and learned the basics of publishing. Franklin also started to write for his brother's newspaper. These experiences helped Franklin develop his talents into the skills that made his great contributions possible.

Greene analyzes more masters that followed a similar approach. Johann Wolfgang von Goethe and Albert Einstein, as well living masters such as Bill Gates, Paul Graham, and Daniel Everett, and many more. For all of these masters, Greene can show how they went through an apprenticeship before they were able to achieve their great accomplishments, sometimes as a literal apprenticeship, but often as a time of intense learning, self-education, and work in a related field. Of course, Greene's approach is prone to the confirmation bias – the neglect of disconfirming evidence for evidence that fits an already existing theory. Nonetheless, Greene is anxious to keep his analysis as scientific as possible.

While Greene's analysis has its flaws, he manages to prove his thesis that skill doesn't simply come to be but needs to be developed methodically. There is not a single case of disconfirming evidence where genius was created without putting in the necessary work. Other scientific concepts of skill, for example, the idea that it takes 10,000 hours of practice to master any skill, seem to confirm Greene's point.

The idea of an apprenticeship is simple, but elegant, and helps us understand what it takes to succeed in life: a lot of initial work without an immediate reward. The apprenticeship is the toughest phase on our way to developing our talents. It is where we understand how much effort it will take, and that it will be a long time before we can reap the rewards. This creates a dangerous imbalance in our four essential needs:

- We have to put in a lot of work without having any guarantee for success. Therefore, our need for certainty encourages us to quit the apprenticeship.
- Many of our family, friends, and peers will encourage us to accept reality and take a secure job that, at the moment, pays more. Therefore, our need for love/connection encourages us to quit the apprenticeship as well.
- Most of the time, our apprenticeship requires us to go through a learning period with lower income and lower social status than if we took the best job currently available. Therefore, our need for significance urges us to quit the apprenticeship, too.
- If we abandon the apprenticeship and take the highest paying job we can get, we can buy the things we dreamed of in all these years in school and college. Therefore, our need for possibility wants us to quit the apprenticeship, too.

These negative feelings towards the apprenticeship cover all four of our essential needs, the basis for our daily decision-making process. Without passion, there's little we have to counter these negative feelings. This explains why passion is so essential for success: passion helps us make it through the apprentice phase without succumbing to the temptation of instant gratification, of taking the seemingly safe way out. Our passion for what we do can replace the needs we fail to satisfy and makes the apprenticeship intrinsically rewarding:

- We work at something we love – we feel love/connection.
- We know that we will always work at what we love and that we will never hate our job – we feel certainty.
- We know that the work we do increases our potential to contribute to what we are passionate about – we feel possibility.
- We contribute to what we care about – we feel significance.

During the initial learning phase, passion gives us the reward we would lack without passion. Without passion, all our essential needs would urge us to quit the apprenticeship – we would only encounter negative emotions and would never be able to make it through.

Passion offers another advantage: most likely we have already started our apprenticeship when we were young. When we are deeply in love with a certain value, we have already used our talents to contribute to this value, simply because this was the best way we knew to deal with what we were interested in. Therefore, we have already completed a part of our apprenticeship; we have already developed our talents to some extent. Now, as we want to use our talents to live our passions, we still need to put the finishing touches on our skill development, but we have already created a basis to start from, a basis that makes the entire process quicker, easier, and more enjoyable. Compared to those of us who choose a career without passion, we have a significant head start on our skill development.

2. Creative-active phase

After a while, the time and the effort we invested in our apprenticeship start to pay dividends. We understand the field we are trying to master; we see connections we were unable to see before, and we can use our new knowledge to contribute more. The creative-active phase is where our unique genetic potential starts to show. When we contribute to our field, we can do so in our own way, combining all our different passions and skills. The result will be similar to what has been there before but at the same time uniquely ours.

- Leonardo da Vinci entered the creative-active phase after he had left Verrocchio's workshop and started to work on his own.
- Charles Darwin entered the creative-active phase when he had returned from his voyage on the Beagle and sat down to classify the results of his trip and complete his theory.
- Benjamin Franklin entered the creative-active phase when he started publishing his newspaper, *The Pennsylvania Gazette*.

For authors, the creative-active phase is the time when they write their first book, for musicians when they write their first songs, for engineers when they create their first project. These first works might not be revolutionary, but they are a necessary step to mastery. They help us make a name for ourselves, accelerate the learning process, and provide us with a deeper understanding of our field.

3. Mastery

Mastery is the perfection of the creative-active phase. Through years of dedicated work, our understanding of our field has become gradually wider and deeper. Eventually, we can make connections beyond single points; we understand the field as a whole. This is mastery.

In our everyday lives, we all encounter glimpses of mastery. In these moments, we know exactly what will happen, how a problem was created, and how to solve it. We have a complete understanding of this one, brief moment, which gives us the ultimate power to handle the situation perfectly. Once the moment is over, we lose this power. Once again we encounter situations we fail to understand completely and where we lack the perfect answer to every problem. According to Greene, mastery is the extension of these brief moments of absolute power to an everlasting control of every situation in our field. What's fleeting to most people becomes a power at our command, a power that we can use as we desire.

> Self-Help Deception #24: We can become masters in any field. (The truth: Mastery can never be reached without passion, which significantly limits the areas where we can achieve it.)

What can we learn from masters?

Even though they lived in different times, different parts of the world, and different social, political, and cultural environments, the lives of people who reached a high level of skill in their fields show some commonalities. These masters started with youthful passion and after a while entered an apprenticeship that helped them learn the basics of their fields. Then they used this knowledge to contribute to the field in a creative way and, after years of practice, achieved mastery, a complete understanding of their fields. This process is only possible because, along the entire way, passion helped them work harder and put in more time than anybody else. From these life paths, we can deduct some interesting conclusions about how to develop our skills:

- There are no shortcuts to developing our skills. The effortless path is a lie. When we lose ourselves in fantasies of quick fixes, we ignore the one power we truly have: developing skill by allowing our passions to fuel our work.
- Neither passion nor skill nor hard work is solely responsible for success in any field of life. Oversimplified, non-reflective self-help books that take a small aspect of success and make it out to be the entire thing or any other theory similarly distracting from reality can cause only harm.

- When we try to skip a step in the process of developing our talents, or when we try to move to its end by applying some magic formula, we move against the true nature of skill. We enter a dead end and only delay the process. Life will pass us by, and true skill will keep alluding us. After a while, we will start to lose faith in ever developing our skills and give up. Then, we become stuck in dead-end careers, feel ashamed for our failure, and create false replacements.

- The true enemies of success are oversimplification, convenience, and lack of passion and skill. When we are too dispassionate about a topic to make it through the apprenticeship and hold course during the creative-active phase, we can never develop our talents. At some point along the way, we succumb to the dangers of instant gratification, of trying to satisfy our needs the quick and easy way.

Self-Help Deception #25: There is a magic formula to accelerate success.

Conclusion

1. It takes work and time to develop our talents into masterful skills. We first need to learn the basics of our field and then need to apply what we learned for years before we can reach mastery.
2. Passion is necessary to help us survive the initial non-rewarding learning phase without taking the easy way out and pursuing instant gratification. Passion multiplies skill.
3. We can't all reach the high levels of Darwin or da Vinci, but since we all have talents and passions, we can make the most of what we have by following a similar approach to life.

Further reading

Robert Greene: Mastery.

A detailed analysis of how masters have developed and then used their strength to contribute to the values they were passionate about and how we can do the same. Though not always scientifically accurate, Greene's book is nonetheless a good guide on how to use passion to develop talents into strengths.

Chapter 11

How can we show more self-control?

„Self-control is the chief element in self-respect.
THUCYDIDES

When I wrote this book, I worked for 12 hours a day. Of these 12 hours, I spent 10 hours writing and wasted 2 hours on social media, YouTube, and mobile games – a 5:1 ratio, not bad. My self-control when writing far exceeds my self-control in any other field. When I wrote papers in college, I wasted almost all my time until the deadline pressured me to reach a 50:50 ratio of work and wasted time. When I did an internship, I hardly worked at all, even though the tasks were mundane and I would probably have enjoyed them. All the way, I saw my co-workers, fellow students, and friends struggle with similar problems. Why is it so hard to show self-control? How are we supposed to follow long term goals if we are unable to control what we do right now? And how can we maximize self-control?

Self-help tries to increase self-control with such techniques as making lists or visualizing goals. Do these techniques work? Psychological studies can help us find better ways to maximize our self-control potential. Let's see what science has to say.

What do we know about self-control?

Pursuing long-term goals that give our day-to-day activities intrinsic meaning helps us to be happy. Nonetheless, pursuing long-term goals is difficult – life often gets in the way. Every one of us knows this situation: we are committed to a long-term goal, but a brief temptation tricks us into doing the exact opposite of what would aid this goal:

- We want to lose weight, but we eat an entire pizza - and we weren't even hungry.
- We want to get work done, but we waste our time on the internet.
- We want to save money, but we keep buying things we do not need.

To create a philosophy of life worth having, we need to get these problems in check. When we are unable to control our behavior, any attempt at creating better lives is doomed to fail.

Too little self-control is one of the main factors why people underachieve – it can even cause violence and other destructive behavior. Most people do not want to hit their children or partners, but after a hard day at work, they get angry and lose control. Similarly, many crimes happen when people lack the self-control to resist stealing an unattended bag or to refuse to relieve their anger by destroying their ex's car.

A lack of self-control always arises from the same type of problem: a *dual-motive conflict*. We have two conflicting goals and our minds fight about which goal to follow right now.

- We want to lose weight, but we also want to eat pizza.
- We want to write a paper, but we also want to check Facebook.
- We want to be financially smart, but we also want a new car.
- We want to stop smoking, but we also want a cigarette.
- We want to be honest, but it would be so much more comfortable to lie.

These conflicts are so difficult because they feature two different kinds of goals. On the one hand, there is a big, highly rewarding long-term goal, such as not dying from lung cancer. On the other hand, there is a much smaller short-term reward, such as a cigarette. Analyzed logically, giving up the short-term reward for pursuing the much bigger long-term goal is an easy decision. Most of us, however, fail on their long-term goals because we keep stumbling from one short-term goal to another. Every time, we only take a small step away from our long-term goal, but these small steps accumulate to a huge distance.

Many self-help books try to solve this problem by simply encouraging us to focus on long-term goals. Maybe they even provide techniques to make the process easier, such as visualizing our long-term goal every morning or keeping a goal journal. Aside from the fact that these techniques are designed to merge our idealized self with our actual self, which reduces our ability to evaluate the world realistically and is one of the main criteria of narcissism, books that promote these techniques fail to answer the big question any valid philosophy of life must answer: why do we need small rewards in the first place? Why do we need the small joy of smoking a cigarette or eating pizza so desperately that we willingly sacrifice our highly rewarding long-term goal of being healthy? What void in our lives are we trying to fill with food and nicotine? Self-help ignores the source of these problems and is, therefore, incapable of delivering a valid plan to solve them.

Self-Help Deception #26: We can switch our attention from short-term distractions to long-term goals at will.

A good philosophy of life eliminates the need for short-term distractions by providing a way of life that in itself is so rewarding that it renders additional perks unnecessary.

- Creating a life that keeps us so happy and engaged in the things we love that we feel no need to add joy by eating is a more constructive solution than using a technique to suppress our desire for pizza.
- Making our tasks and goals so intrinsically rewarding that we feel no need to be distracted from them by social media, TV, etc. is a more constructive solution than employing a complicated technique to keep track of extrinsic tasks and goals.

Short-term goals often overrule long-term goals because these two types of goals differ in more respects than their time scale. Short-term goals are specific. We know exactly what we get: that pizza, that cigarette, that TV show. Long-term goals, however, are abstract: losing weight, stopping smoking, and being happy – we wonder exactly what we will get, whether we will get it, and what it takes to get there. As a result, short-term goals are more attractive to us in every single situation. They are closer and stronger; they feel more real. Goals that are in the distant future *feel* less attractive, less important, and less influential, even if they *are* the exact opposite.

> „The consequence of a person's actions seem less important the further the consequences are in the future."
>
> MARK LEARY

Psychologists call this effect *temporal discounting*. We discount what's further in the future. Researchers made test subjects choose between a lower reward now and a higher reward in the future. They could either have $900 now or $1,000 in six months. Logic dictates to take the higher reward, but many people feel tempted to take the $900 now because they discount the value of the money six months later. The same mechanism translates to all aspects of our lives – rewards and punishments seem less significant if they are in the distant future. If someone had to decide between smoking a cigarette and dying from cancer immediately, nobody would ever smoke. But since the horrible consequence is far away, people often discount it and smoke anyway. When people suffer serious consequences from smoking – a stroke, a heart attack, cancer – this changes. Then, the threat is closer and more real to them. Now, these people have no trouble quitting smoking. Unfortunately, it is often too late. Similarly, finding a partner we love could take years, and we can never be sure to achieve this goal. Having sex with a stranger is much less rewarding but also specific and near, which is why we sometimes make the mistake to prefer this less rewarding goal.

In conclusion, there are three reasons why self-control is so difficult:

- Abstract rewards (health, happiness, love, etc.) are less attractive than specific rewards (pizza, TV, sex, etc.).

- Future consequences and rewards seem to be less important than immediate consequences and rewards.
- Our most important goals are abstract and distant and often opposed to our short-term goals.

Why is self-control so hard?

Pursuing long-term goals is important for a good, happy life, even though they are more abstract and lie further in the future. But can we start moving towards long-term goals by simply ignoring short-term distractions, by simply strengthening our will and focusing on what we want, as self-help literature suggests? Unfortunately, things aren't that simple. As we saw in chapter 2 ("What makes us happy?"), a significant part of happiness depends on doing things that have intrinsic value to us, that are rewarding right now. Doing things only because we hope they create a better future is not intrinsically rewarding and fails to make us happy.

This dilemma is a problem. On first sight it seems as if we have to choose between being care-free fun lovers who have a great time now but will never accomplish anything, and boring hard workers who neglect all our desires, hoping to achieve a greater goal decades from now. Most people fall for this misconception, devoting their younger years to short-term fun and their later years to boring work.

This solution is far from ideal for a couple of reasons:

1. In both their youth and their later years, these people feel that they are missing something. By focusing on one extreme, they neglect everything else. To be truly happy, we need fun *and* long term goals.
2. It is impossible to change completely who we are in the midst of life. When we focus on fun in our early adult lives and try to switch our entire personality after we graduate from college, turn 30, or reach some other arbitrary point that we declare to be the beginning of seriousness, everything we know becomes worthless. We face a new world where none of our skills help us achieve the outcome we want. We can only fail. To have some positive emotions, we are bound to slide back to what we know. Those of us who suffer most from this problem end up as 40- or 50-year-olds who still feel and act like 20-year olds, terrified of getting older.

The main problem in this dilemma is that most people distinguish between things that are fun and things that have long-term value. We can make self-control a great deal easier by doing things that are fun *and* have long-term value. Then, we can align our short-term goals with our long-term goals and no longer have to choose between two types of rewards – we can have both. Living our true selves helps us with this approach by aligning our essential needs with our non-essential needs. Nonetheless, while living our true selves can make self-control easier, it fails to cure all problems:

- In some areas of life, doing what has little intrinsic value to us is unavoidable. We have to pay taxes, do chores around the house, or drive to work, whether we like it or not.
- Even if we only do what has intrinsic value to us, we still need self-control to focus on the task at hand – we might need less, but we always need some self-control.

Managing our self-control well can help us deal with these problems.

How to show more self-control

Ask yourself: at what time of day is your self-control at its lowest? When do you tend to overeat, for example? In the morning or in the evening? For most people it is in the evening. Psychologists have an interesting explanation for this behavior: they discovered that self-control works like a muscle. When a muscle is rested, it performs at maximum strength. The more we use the muscle, the weaker it gets. The same applies to self-control. Researchers made people do two tasks that require self-control. The subjects did worse on the second test, regardless of which tests they had to do and in which order they had to do them. The subjects had used a part of their self-control power in the first test, and, as a result of their depleted resources, found it difficult to exercise the same level of self-control on the second test. Researchers concluded that we can create better, happier lives by eliminating anything that is unnecessary:

- When we waste all our self-control on marginal tasks, we have no self-control left for what's important to us, even if we love these tasks.
- Forcing us to do things we have no desire to do takes more power out of our self-control battery than focusing on what we love. Even a few tasks we hate can render us useless for the rest of the day.

We can get more things done if we focus on what has intrinsic value to us and eliminate everything else. To waste less self-control on the things we are unable to eliminate – filing tax returns, doing chores, driving to work – we can find a way to integrate them into our intrinsic goals or outsource them.

- We can pay someone to do our taxes.
- While we drive to work, we can listen to an audio book about a topic we love, thereby adding intrinsic value to our commute.
- As a writer, I use doing chores to get a much-needed break from work. I take out the garbage, clean the bathroom, or get my books in order to

overcome writer's block. This strategy adds intrinsic value to activities I otherwise consider a waste of time.

We can be much happier doing less. When we accumulate too many responsibilities, we have to do more extrinsic things and drain our self-control batteries. Without self-control, we are unable to focus, even on what has intrinsic value to us. We feel tired, have to go to bed early, or rest on the couch.

As soon as we recognize that a task drains our self-control batteries but fails to contribute to what we are passionate about, we are better off quitting it. Many of us have allowed fear, insecurity, and the need for approval to trick ourselves into taking on too many responsibilities. We work a full-time job, constantly overworking ourselves to please the boss; we are members of 5 clubs, the PTA, and a charity organization, and also try to keep up time-consuming hobbies. These lives are exhausting and stop us from developing long-lasting happiness. Focusing on what's important to us and thereby eliminating battery draining activities increases our ability to show self-control and helps us lead better lives.

Self-Help Deception #27: We can create better lives by taking on more responsibilities and by investing more time.

These findings also apply to charity work. Charity organizations prefer money donations that allow them to hire skilled long-term employees over having a different unskilled volunteer every day. When we save time by not doing charity work and use a part of this time to make money to donate, we will be happier, feel more fulfilled, *and* benefit charity more. Volunteering should be left to superstars who can command media attention. For anyone else, it is a false replacement for a lack of love/connection and significance.

Conclusion

1. Self-control is difficult because short-term distractions feel more real to our brain than long-term goals, which we discount. In situations with a dual-motive conflict, we are likely to prefer the short-term distraction over the long-term goal.
2. Self-control works like a muscle – the more we use it, the less effective it becomes.
3. To avoid wasting all our self-control on meaningless activities, we have three options:
   a) Focus on activities with intrinsic value,
   b) Eliminate unnecessary tasks and commitments, and
   c) Take time off to allow our self-control to recover.

Further reading

Roy F. Baumeister & John Tierney: Willpower. Rediscovering the Greatest Human Strength.

Research psychologist Roy F. Baumeister and *New York Times* science writer John Tierney present the newest research on self-control and strategies on how we can manage our self-control better.

Leo Babauta – The Power of Less.

A great guide to eliminating unnecessary activities that only drain our self-control batteries and make us unhappy.

Chapter 12

Do we need self-esteem to lead good lives?

For the last few decades, self-esteem has been considered one of the most positive character traits, with some psychologists promoting it as the cure-all for many mental problems. American psychologist Nathaniel Branden, the author of many books about the value of self-esteem and techniques to increase self-esteem, wrote:

> „ *Self-esteem has profound implications for every aspect of our existence ... I can't think of a single psychological problem – from anxiety and depression ... to spouse battering or child molestation to co-dependency and sexual disorders, to passivity and chronic aimlessness, to suicide and crimes of violence – that is not traceable, at least in part, to the problem of deficient self-esteem."*
>
> NATHANIEL BRANDEN

Branden's colleague, the American sociologist Neil Smelser, even suggested that many problems in society – crime, drugs, and welfare dependency, among others – can be cured by increasing self-esteem. In line with this belief, the state of California started a campaign to raise self-esteem in the 1980s, hoping for impacts as far reaching as a balanced state budget. Self-help books, too, played a great role in promoting self-esteem as an important factor for success and happiness, with many authors elevating self-esteem to an essential quality, a necessary ingredient for success in every aspect of life.

This high praise for self-esteem raises two questions:

1. Is self-esteem truly as important to our lives as these claims indicate?
2. If it is, why?

By answering these two questions, we can decide whether a scientifically sound philosophy of life has to include high self-esteem as an essential ingredient.

What is self-esteem?

Many of us have a vague definition of self-esteem. Without a concrete concept that could distinguish self-esteem from our confidence to do basic activities, the resulting blurry lines make discussing self-esteem difficult – a fact that has led to many misconceptions. In psychology, self-esteem defines how well we generally feel about who we are and what we do. This definition clearly distinguishes self-esteem from self-confidence, which describes the belief that we can perform a specific activity or generate a certain outcome. Self-esteem is a general feeling; self-confidence is tied to a specific situation or activity. We can have low self-esteem, but still have high self-confidence. Even people with almost no self-esteem have high self-confidence when it comes to basic activities such as brushing their teeth, walking, or speaking. In this chapter, we focus on self-esteem, not self-confidence.

Psychologists distinguish between two types of self-esteem:

1. *Trait self-esteem* describes how good we feel about ourselves in general. When people talk about self-esteem, they usually mean trait self-esteem.
2. *Situational self-esteem* describes how good we feel about ourselves right now. People with high trait self-esteem can feel pretty bad about themselves because of something they did or something that happened to them. While our trait self-esteem remains fairly constant, our situational self-esteem fluctuates.

With this definition of self-esteem, we can analyze how self-esteem influences our lives. Those who promote self-esteem as the key to a good life invoke two hypotheses:

- High self-esteem makes people happier and more successful.
- High self-esteem leads to positive emotions and behavior.

To find out whether these claims are true, let's look at the proof that the promoters of high self-esteem put forward. Research seems to suggest a strong connection between self-esteem and desirable character traits and life events.

People with high self-esteem are ...

- Better students – they have better grades and a lower dropout rate, and they are better educated overall.
- Less prone to addiction – they are less likely to abuse alcohol or drugs.
- Happier – they are more likely to be happy with their lives and less likely to become depressed.
- More mentally stable – they are less likely to be neurotic, anxious, or worried.
- More successful in their jobs – they hold higher positions and make more money.

These findings contrast with what we know about people with low self-esteem.

People with low self-esteem are ...

- Less honest,
- More likely to become criminals,
- More likely to join gangs,
- More likely to underachieve,

- More likely to fail at what they want to do,
- More neurotic,
- More likely to have unwanted pregnancies.

For the most part, self-esteem is not the main correlating factor for people who develop these positive or negative characteristics, but there is a significant, consistent correlation between high self-esteem and positive characteristics and between low self-esteem and negative characteristics.

These correlations have led generations of psychologists and self-help writers to conclude that high self-esteem is important, assuming that higher self-esteem promotes positive characteristics while lower self-esteem leads to negative characteristics. On first thought, this conclusion seems to be reasonable and based on plenty of evidence. On second thought, however, this conclusion neglects the important question whether self-esteem is the cause or the effect of these characteristics. American psychologist Mark Leary, who has researched the influence of self-esteem on our lives in great detail, discovered that the relationship between self-esteem and positive characteristics is not what it seems.[1]

Does high self-esteem create better lives?

In itself, correlation is meaningless. From 1999 to 2009, the U.S. spending on science, space, and technology has correlated strongly with the number of suicides by hanging, strangulation, and suffocation.[2] But does that mean that one causes the other? No. When we find a correlation, we have to make sure this correlation is not just a coincidence, and if it is not, we have to determine which of the involved criteria is the cause and which is the effect.

In the same way, we have to determine whether self-esteem truly causes positive and negative characteristics. Only then we can decide whether we can improve our lives by increasing our self-esteem. Elevating self-esteem to a "magic bullet" simply because there is a correlation is unscientific – regardless of how well it may fit the dominant self-help narrative.

Psychologists such as Mark Leary have researched the influence of self-esteem on our lives for decades. Their overwhelming answer is: low self-esteem doesn't appear to cause negative effects in our lives, and high self-esteem doesn't appear to cause positive effects in our lives.

So how can we explain the strong correlation between high or low self-esteem and good or bad character traits and events? Well, there is only one logical explanation: if self-esteem is not the cause, self-esteem has to be the effect. This is exactly what research has shown:

---

[1] For the original article read: Mark R. Leary: Making Sense of Self-Esteem, in: Current Directions in Psychological Science 8 (1), 1999, p. 32–35. The article is available online, and Google will find it.
[2] For the exact data go to: http://tylervigen.com/view_correlation?id=1597

- Students do not do well in school because they have higher self-esteem. Academic success causes higher self-esteem.
- People with low self-esteem do not abuse alcohol and drugs. Abusing alcohol and drugs causes low self-esteem.
- Low self-esteem doesn't cause mental illnesses. Mental illnesses and the events that create them cause lower self-esteem.
- People with low self-esteem do not become more neurotic. Neurotic people have lower self-esteem.
- Low self-esteem doesn't cause unwanted pregnancies. Unwanted pregnancies cause low self-esteem.

While many self-help books and life-coaches promote self-esteem as the answer to all our problems, there's almost no scientific evidence that self-esteem has any influence on our lives. Studies that focused on changes in self-esteem over time show that positive or negative events precede changes in self-esteem, not the other way around. In fact, we can easily explain why undesirable emotions and behavior correlate with low self-esteem:

- Low self-esteem is a reaction to rejection or feelings of inadequacy. When people get rejected or feel inadequate, low self-esteem is not the only feeling they experience. They feel hurt, angry, jealous, ashamed, etc. These negative emotions can cause false replacements. Low self-esteem is not the cause of these negative emotions, low self-esteem, and negative emotions are both effects of the same cause.
- Many forms of negative behavior create rejection and low self-esteem. Most mental illnesses, addictions, or negative character traits cause others to distance themselves from us. This rejection lowers our self-esteem. In this case, lower self-esteem is the effect of undesirable behavior, not the other way around.
- Lower self-esteem increases our desire to be accepted. Usually, people try to find acceptance through desirable behavior – being nice, helping others, etc. This doesn't work for some people, however, for whatever reason. Deprived of any opportunity to find acceptance through doing good, some of these people seize illegal and immoral ways to gain acceptance – they lie, steal, or cheat. Some might join anti-social groups where the threshold for acceptance is lower. In this case, low self-esteem is a factor in causing destructive behavior, but only a minor factor that has been preceded by more important reasons. Raising self-esteem would fail to solve the problem.

Self-Help Deception #28: Increasing self-esteem can help us lead better lives.

What does self-esteem do?

We all have a strong desire to have high self-esteem. If self-esteem doesn't cause positive effects in our lives, then why do we want to have high self-esteem at all? Evolution has optimized our chances to survive and reproduce, so self-esteem must have some psychological effect that helps us in this respect. But what? To answer this question, psychologists created a concept called *sociometer theory*. They understood that, if self-esteem is the effect of our behavior but has no direct influence on what we do, self-esteem works like a gauge. According to sociometer theory, self-esteem measures how much we are appreciated or rejected by others. Self-esteem measures the satisfaction of our needs for love/connection and significance.

In this gauge, state self-esteem determines whether the needle is currently moving up or down. Trait self-esteem determines the needle's resting point. We are genetically equipped with a base level of self-esteem, our trait self-esteem. Through our actions, we can increase our state self-esteem and influence our genetic predisposition. When we experience high or low state self-esteem for a long time, our trait self-esteem begins to move in this direction, too. Mark Leary related self-esteem to a gas gauge in a car. Instead of monitoring how much gas is in our tank, self-esteem monitors to what extent other people value or devalue us. This scientifically sound concept is fundamentally different from what most self-help books tell us about self-esteem – it redefines everything.

As human beings, we depend on the acceptance of others. Throughout evolution, those humans who were abandoned by their group had little chance to survive and procreate. We needed a group to provide us with food and shelter, to take care of us when we are sick, and to meet members of the other sex. Those humans who were better suited to live in groups were more likely to pass on their genes. In our modern times, belonging to a group is no longer necessary for survival. Society provides us with food, shelter, and medical care, even if we are not particularly likable or skilled. Nonetheless, we carry the same genes that helped our ancestors survive. As a result, we still feel the need to belong to a large social construct.

Self-esteem is the gauge that helps us monitor our social acceptance, and, by emitting hormones that make us feel better when we are accepted, self-esteem motivates us to fit in with others. Self-esteem is supposed to make sure that we behave in ways that others find acceptable, and that we neither do nor think what could cause others to leave us on our own, with no chance to procreate. When members of our social group indicate that what we do increases our value in their eyes, our self-esteem goes up. We feel better about ourselves, and we are motivated to keep doing what we are doing. When others indicate that what we do decreases our value in their eyes, our self-esteem decreases and we feel worse about ourselves – we are motivated to change in a way that helps us fit in with the group.

Researchers have tested and proved this relation many times. When they led test subjects to believe that others rejected them or that they failed, the test subjects' state self-esteem went down. When researchers led test subjects to believe that others approved of them or that they succeeded, the test subjects' state self-esteem went up. In a similar study, researchers gave test subjects a list of behaviors. The subjects had to rate how good they would feel about themselves if they engaged in a certain behavior and how good they would expect others to feel about them. The results were conclusive: people felt good about themselves when they expected others to feel good about them. If they expected others to disapprove of their behavior, they felt worse about themselves. Knowing that their behavior could cause rejection made them feel bad. These results apply to all mentally healthy human beings – we all care what others think about us, and self-esteem is the gauge that measures how well we are doing. While some people claim that they are indifferent to what other people think of them and that other people's opinions have no influence on their self-esteem, that is simply not true. Studies have conclusively proven that all healthy people are concerned with what others think of them. How good or bad we feel about ourselves in a given situation largely depends on how good or bad others think about us.

Can we improve our lives by raising self-esteem artificially?

If self-esteem is only a gauge, would there be any harm in trying to artificially increase our self-esteem to feel better? Would feeling better lead to a better life, as many self-help books suggest? Research indicates it would not. There are six reasons why artificially increased self-esteem fails to improve our quality of life.

1. Self-esteem is only one of many factors in every decision.

Self-esteem is only one of many factors in any decision-making process. Focusing on raising self-esteem takes our focus away from where we need it more. This is where Leary's gas gauge analogy comes fully into play. Much like a gas gauge, self-esteem only indicates what is happening. How we react to this indication depends on other factors that are more important than the indication itself.

In every situation, we factor self-esteem into our decision-making process. How likely will others approve or disapprove of different possible options? How do we feel about ourselves right now? When we have low self-esteem, for example, we are more likely to do what we think can give us a boost in self-esteem.

How we try to increase our self-esteem, however, is far more important than the fact that we try to increase it – we can try to cure cancer or to steal a Rolex. In any decision-making process, there are far more important factors than self-esteem.

2. There is no shortage of self-esteem.

When we talk about high or low self-esteem in people, we talk about a relative value compared to the average person. In this range, however, even relatively low self-esteem means that people have an overall medium level of self-esteem.

Only very few people suffer from generally low self-esteem. Most of us have certain characteristics that we think make us likable – which gives us, at least, a moderate level of self-esteem – or feel generally good about themselves – which creates high self-esteem. If you are not mentally ill, you are very unlikely to suffer from low self-esteem.

3. Realism trumps high self-esteem.

Researchers started to record self-esteem in widespread analyses in the 1960s. Since then, the level of trait self-esteem in people has increased continuously. Culture, parents, and teachers have bought into the myth that high self-esteem will help us lead better lives, which translates to how we raise our children.

Despite of this rise in self-esteem, children today are more likely to commit crimes than in the 1960s, they are more likely to abuse alcohol and drugs, they are more likely to be depressed, drop out of school, etc. While young people's self-esteem is rising, they are not leading better lives.

We can make the best decisions when our level of self-esteem reflects our true situation, skills, and possibilities. We need to see the world as it is, any distortion from reality hurts us. When we consider ourselves better or worse than we are, we make bad decisions that decrease our quality of life and can lead to undesirable behavior.

4. Promoting self-esteem is faulty logic.

Most self-help books focus on high self-esteem as a positive quality because they succumb to the survivorship bias. Seeing many successful people with high self-esteem can easily trick us into thinking that high self-esteem leads to success. In fact, though, we simply focus on the small minority of people who have the impressive skills to justify their abnormally high level of self-esteem. When these people consider their abilities above average, they are not artificially confident, they are *right* – through realistic self-evaluation, their impressive skill-level has led to high self-esteem. The overwhelming majority of people who artificially increase their self-esteem without the necessary skills, however, end up unhappy, disenchanted, and often made fun of. They would have been better off getting by with the self-esteem their life-situation naturally generated. When it comes to self-evaluation, the key to a good life is realism, not high self-esteem.

5. Too high self-esteem stops us from creating a better life.

To stay with Leary's gas gauge analogy, artificially increasing the gas gauge's reading fails to solve our problem if we are low on gas. It can only cloud our awareness and distract us from doing what is reasonable. The same applies to self-esteem. To effectively deal with life's challenges, we need a realistic picture of ourselves, a reasonable evaluation of our strengths and weaknesses. If we want to feel better about who we are, if we want to increase self-esteem, we have to become better people and create a better life. Then others will react more positively to us, and our self-esteem will increase, too. Artificially increasing our self-esteem can only distract us from this healthy process.

6. Artificially increasing our self-esteem creates more problems than it solves.

While artificially increasing our self-esteem fails to provide positive effects, it does have negative consequences that will reduce the quality and happiness of our lives:

- When we have higher self-esteem than is reasonable, we will constantly be faced with people who seemingly fail to recognize how wonderful we are, making us angry and irritable. In the worst case, we become narcissists.
- Too high self-esteem reduces our desire to improve ourselves. To improve where necessary, we realistically need to understand our strengths and weaknesses.
- Overestimating ourselves gets us into situations that are beyond our capabilities, situations that require as much skill as we believe we have, but far more than we actually have. Overblown self-esteem increases our chances of failure, rejection, and shame.
- Often, we do not truly believe the positive image we are trying to convey. Secretly, we know that we are not as good as we are trying to make others believe, not even as good as we want to be or think we ought to be. As a result, we feel shame and create false replacements.

Self-Help Deception #29: Higher self-esteem is more desirable than lower self-esteem.

Conclusion

1. Self-esteem is a gauge that measures how well others accept us – how well our needs for love/connection and significance are met.
2. It makes more sense to prevent the negative events that lead to low self-esteem than to artificially increase self-esteem – it is better to fix the problem than to manipulate the gauge.
3. Artificially increasing self-esteem has no positive effects but leads to some negative consequences. To create a good life, it is essential to evaluate ourselves as reasonably and realistically as possible.

Further reading

Sociometer Theory and the Pursuit of Relational Value: Getting to the Root of Self-Esteem, European Review of Social Psychology 16, no 3, 2005, 75-111.

The true nature of self-esteem explained in less than 40 pages – a quick and insightful read on why we want to have high self-esteem.

Roy F. Baumeister et al.: Exploding the Self-Esteem Myth, Scientific American 292, no 1, 84-91.

An article detailing the misconceptions about self-esteem.

Jean M. Twenge & W. Keith Campbell: The Narcissism Epidemic. Living in the Age of Entitlement.

Hard facts and interesting stories about how our lives tend to be more and more influenced by narcissism, the negative effects of this development, and what we can do to stop it. A great, highly recommendable read for anyone who wants to stop too high self-esteem from creating an inner prison.

Chapter 13

How to evaluate ourselves reasonably

One of my worst experiences in politics happened in my second year of college. In the first session of my assignment to the committee for youth development of the city of Jena, we discussed how to distribute the budget. There was a long line of projects and institutions that presented us their ideas and it was our job to decide which projects got funded and which did not. To make a good decision, I would have needed a solid understanding of the facilities' neighborhoods and their development over the last few years. I, however, had moved to Jena only one year earlier and would have been incapable of pointing at these neighborhoods on a map. Since this was a time before smartphones, there was no opportunity to research information while the meeting progressed. Clueless and confused, I had to decide about the future of youth programs and the kids in them. There were only five members on the committee, so my vote was important. With the other members' help, I made the best of the situation, but there was little doubt that I was completely out of place. If I had evaluated myself reasonably, I would have known that it was impossible to understand the complex connections of a city's neighborhoods in a few evenings of study. I overestimated my abilities and wasted my time in an effort that was doomed to fail. How could I have evaluated myself more reasonably?

As research confirms, a spot-on self-evaluation is difficult. Self-help encourages us to avoid a realistic self-evaluation in favor of a limitless belief in our abilities – an approach that, as we have seen, leads to more problems than it solves. How can we do it better? Let's see which challenges we encounter when evaluating ourselves and how we can overcome them.

Why we fail to evaluate ourselves reasonably

To determine how reasonably people evaluate themselves, researchers carried out large surveys and asked their test subjects simple questions such as these:

Compared to the average person of your age, how do you assess yourself in the following aspects?

- How safe a driver are you?
- How good a friend are you?
- How honest are you?
- How good a job do you do at work?
- How intelligent are you?

Statistical data tells us that the distribution of almost every skill and characteristic follows a bell-shaped curve, as in the picture below. Most people are somewhere near the average, and a few people are spread to each end, either better or worse than the average. If we evaluated ourselves reasonably, most test subjects should have answered that they are about average on every question, while the number of people who think that they are above or below average should be roughly the same.

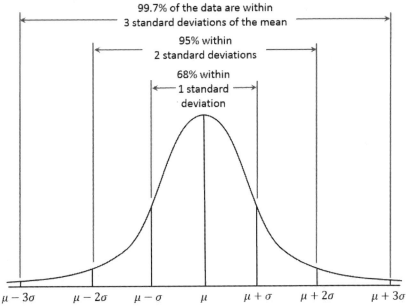

The actual results, however, differed greatly from this prediction. On almost every question, a high percentage of people assessed their skills as above average. In one test with 40 questions, the majority of people assessed themselves as above average on 38 of 40 questions.

Apparently, we tend to overestimate ourselves, often heavily. In an Australian study, 86 percent of employees said that they do a better job than the average employee while only 1 percent said that they do a worse job. Many employees obviously have an exaggerated opinion of themselves. Psychologists call this kind of phenomenon a *self-serving bias* – we tend to overestimate our abilities.

While Self-help books often argue that we sell ourselves short and could lead better lives by considering our abilities more highly, there is no evidence to confirm these claims. We tend to overestimate ourselves, and we do not need any additional encouragement to think better about ourselves.

Self-Help Deception #30: Most people underestimate their abilities.

Self-serving biases go even further. We do not only overestimate ourselves, but we also overestimate what's associated with us. We think that our friends, social groups, values, countries, favorite sports teams and favorite musicians are inherently better than other friends, social groups, values, etc. Of course, one could argue that we associate with certain things *because* we value them higher than other things, and that, if we did not value them highly, we would disassociate from them. There are, however, some self-serving biases this theory fails to explain. One of them, the *mere ownership effect*, describes the phenomenon that we value things higher simply because we own them. Once again, one could argue that we simply buy the things we think are best, but there's more to it. One study tested the mere ownership effect by showing test subjects four small objects of similar worth: a pen, a pencil, an eraser, and a ruler, for example. Then they randomly selected one of the objects, gave it to the test person, and asked them to rate the four items again. Surprisingly, the person now rated the object they had received higher than before while they rated all other items the same. Simply owning something increased its perceived value.

With some items, the mere ownership effect is explainable:

- For most of us, our cars are a status symbol, at least, to some extent. Since we worked hard and paid a lot of money to get our cars, it is only natural that we want them to be the best cars we could get. We overlook small deficiencies more willingly than we would with cars that we did not invest that much time and energy in, which makes it easy to overvalue our car.
- The same applies to our jobs. We invest a lot of time and effort into our jobs, and we see every little positive result they generate. This makes it easy to overestimate their worth compared to other jobs.

Once again, though, these theories can only explain part of the problem:

- A fascinating example of the mere ownership effect are the letters in our names. When researchers asked people to rank the letters in the alphabet, they found that people consistently ranked their initials higher than chance would predict. This effect has been found in numerous studies all over the world and even extends to company names – we prefer products from companies with the same initials as our own, and we prefer stocks from companies with the same initials. There is no logical explanation for such behavior.
- Even more significantly, a study by the State University of New York showed that Americans move to cities and states that resemble their own names.[3] There is a higher share of women named Virginia in Virginia than

---

[3] For more information, read: Brett W. Pelham, Matthew C. Mirenberg, and John T. Jones: Why Susie Sells Seashells by the Seashore: Implicit Egotism and Major Life Decisions, State University of

in any other state; there are more Georges in Georgia, and so on. In cities named after a saint, there's a disproportionately high amount of people with the saint's name. There are too many Pauls in St. Paul, too many Luises in St. Louis, and so on. Researchers did their best to account for children being named after their hometown, but the effect was still significant. Compared to what we expect from the average distribution of names, 44 percent more men and women live in cities that are named after a saint with their name.

These effects are important because they are subconscious. Without us noticing it, they subtly influence our behavior. The mere ownership effect helps us understand why someone named Chris feels better about stocks from Coca Cola than about stocks from Pepsi. When we want to buy stocks, we can question whether our hunch is the result of the company's economic power or its name, allowing us to make a better, more rational decision and avoiding a bad investment.

The self-serving bias has more negative consequences. When we succeed, we overestimate our contributions to our success; when we fail, we underestimate our contribution and blame other factors. Looking back on our lives, this distorted way of thinking leads us to overestimate our abilities. Based on such a biased image of our past, we must believe that to have something done right we need to do it ourselves and that we are better and more talented than we are.

What happens when we overestimate ourselves?

We all fall prey to self-serving biases. Even when we are asked how realistically we evaluate ourselves, we show the same bias. Most of us think that we evaluate ourselves more realistically than others. We are biased, and we are biased to think that we are not biased. We naturally believe our self-image is more accurate than most other people's. But is this behavior harmful? Some people argue that having an overly positive view of ourselves helps us to create positive emotions and stay motivated. If we knew how bad we truly are at something, we might stop trying. In their view, the self-serving bias helps us push through obstacles and is helpful.

From an evolutionary point of view, this argument makes sense. Hundreds of thousands of years ago, our ancestors had to hunt animals for food and avoid predators. Those of our ancestors who underestimated themselves and thought that there was no sense in trying had a smaller chance to reproduce than those who always believed in their abilities. Of course,

---

New York at Buffalo. You can find the text on Google.

some of our over-confident ancestors died because they overestimated their skills and acted dangerously, but evolution is indifferent to losers – they never reproduce. Those who did reproduce had a tendency to overestimate themselves. This tendency was passed on and still lives within us today.

In our modern world, our self-serving biases come at a big cost. We are no longer fighting for survival; we are trying to create good lives. This change in our main goal makes the self-serving bias one of the most important causes of problems and unhappiness:

- We manage our lives best when we have a realistic view of what we can do and what we can't do. By making us over-estimate ourselves, the self-serving bias sets us up for failure. We set unrealistic goals and get into situations where we can only fail.

- In some situations, overestimating our abilities can be dangerous. Every year, people die because they overestimated their physical abilities to climb mountains, run marathons, or do other extreme sports. Other people die or ruin their lives because they overestimate their mental abilities to deal with a certain situation. One of the most prominent examples is Christopher McCandless, who starved to death after he moved into the wilderness of Alaska without the necessary survival skills. McCandless' motives were honorable - he wanted to find his true self - but he overestimated his skills and made a hasty decision.[4]

- A too positive self-image can stop us from improving ourselves and correcting problems. When we believe that we are better than average, we are tempted to blame our problems on other, less brilliant people.

- It is true that a positive self-image can help us persevere after failure. But it makes little sense to keep trying to do what we can't do. It would be much better to evaluate our chances to succeed realistically and invest our effort accordingly. Perseverance is not a generally positive characteristic. In fact, perseverance in the face of sure failure is stupid. It is better to understand our limits than to act as if we had none.

- Self-serving biases can damage our social relationships. When we think that we are better than we truly are, we are easily irritated by people who fail to recognize our self-proclaimed glory. We tend to blame others too heavily for our problems, and we undervalue them. Many of our problems arise because we keep insisting that we are better than everyone else.

- When groups are successful, each member tends to put too much emphasis on their contributions. When others get more recognition, these members think that they are undervalued and become jealous. When

---

[4] For more information on McCandless' intriguing story, I recommend Jon Krakauer's book *Into the Wild* or the movie adaption of the same name. Both tell the story of an idealistic, likeable young man who died because he prepared insufficiently - a tragedy we should avoid repeating.

groups underperform, each member places too much blame on the others and feels that they get too much of the blame. Both kinds of behavior are destructive.

- As we will see in Chapter 15 ("How to know what to believe"), self-serving biases are the cause of many conflicts and wars.

Self-Help Deception #31: Perseverance is always a good quality.

When we dive deeper into the nature of self-serving biases, we find an interesting phenomenon: while many of us believe our biases, we often communicate self-serving biases that we do not believe. Studies show that people sometimes claim to be above average in a skill or characteristic but at the same time are insecure about this skill. Apparently, they try to convey a better picture to the outside than they believe. This doesn't apply to all instances of the self-serving bias, but to some of them. We know the ugly truth, that we are not as great as we try to make others believe, but we want to keep it a secret. From an evolutionary position, it makes sense to convey a positive self-image, even if we do not believe in it. When we had to survive in small groups in the wild, we needed others to think highly enough of us to keep us in their group. In our modern society, however, we are no longer at risk of being excluded. Now, the self-serving bias can only do us harm. We feel ashamed for not being as perfect as we claim to be and create false replacements.

How can we fix these problems?

Unfortunately, we can't eliminate the self-serving bias by simply strengthening another characteristic. Some people chronically underestimate themselves, but this behavior is just as hurtful. Nonetheless, the characteristic that seems to correlate the most with a realistic self-image is humility. Humility improves our behavior in some measurable ways:

- Humble people neither undervalue nor overvalue themselves as much. They see themselves more realistically.
- Humble people know what they are good at and what they are bad at. They know which positive and which negative characteristics they have.
- Humble people accept their strengths and weaknesses and are less engaged in creating an overly positive image of themselves.
- When humble people recognize a talent or a positive characteristic about themselves, they keep it in perspective. They know that they are only good at one thing and that this doesn't entitle them to anything or make them a better person. Similarly, humble people do not think they are worthless when they do something wrong. They experience less shame and create fewer false replacements.

The reason humble people handle themselves better seems to be that they do what has intrinsic value to them – they live their true selves. Since what they do is intrinsically rewarding to them, humble people do not need to add extra value to their actions and characteristics, they can accept them for as much or as little as they are. If what we do already has value, we do not need to add to it by overemphasizing ourselves. It seems that a self-serving bias is a false replacement that we create because what we do is not intrinsically rewarding enough to us and we try to add value in some other way. When we do what already is of intrinsic value to us, we are naturally more humble about it, we can trick the self-serving bias, and we can evaluate ourselves more reasonably. A few hundred thousand years ago, this way of thinking might have gotten us expelled from our group. In our modern times, however, humility will greatly increase our happiness.

Self-Help Deception #32: Humility is a sign of weakness and mediocrity.

Conclusion

1. We have a natural tendency to overestimate our characteristics, skills, and contributions, a self-serving bias that creates problems and makes us unhappy.
2. We can overcome our self-serving bias by being humble. Humility increases our quality of life and our happiness.
3. Living our true selves helps us to be humble. When we do what has intrinsic value to us, we do not need to add value by exaggerating ourselves; we already receive enough value from what we do.

Further reading

Mark R. Leary: The Curse of the Self. Self-Awareness, Egotism, and the Quality of Human Life.
Leary provides an insightful look into the human mind, arguing that our egotism decreases the quality of our lives significantly. A good book for everyone who wants to step out of his own way.

James K. Beggan: On the Social Nature of Nonsocial Perception. The Mere Ownership Effect, Journal of Personality and Social Psychology 62 (1992), 229-37.
An article detailing the research behind the mere ownership effect.

Mark D. Alicke, et al.: Personal Contact, Individuation, and the Better-than-Average Effect, Journal of Personality and Social Psychology 68 (1995), 804-25.
The article contains the study where participants rated themselves above average on 38 of 40 traits and other interesting studies of same effect.

Chapter 14

Should we ignore what others think of us?

My grandpa died from a heart attack when my mother was only ten years old. Because he was a hard-working politician, my family attributed his early death to his profession and met my political endeavors with mixed feelings, to say the least. A few times, my grandma went so far as to call me and beg me to stop my madness. When I started playing football, my family reacted similarly. Even though they knew nothing about football and medicine, they were sure that, for someone who had already broken his neck once, playing football was a certain death sentence. I found this situation difficult to deal with. While self-help books encouraged me to ignore other people's opinions and to do what I believed in, having my family constantly remind me how little they valued the two activities that I loved most was hard to dismiss. I found myself trying to ignore what was impossible to ignore, failed, and felt ashamed for my self-perceived weakness.

In the self-help world, people who care what others think of them are often considered weak, inauthentic, and wane. Many self-help books even give advice on how we can get better at ignoring other people's' opinions. But are these claims based on scientific evidence? Does it hurt us to care what others think of us? And are people who ignore the opinions of others really happier and lead better lives?

As it turns out, things are a little more complex. While caring about other people's opinions can sometimes lead to negative emotions, destructive behavior, and unhappiness, trying to ignore others' opinions completely creates more problems than it solves. Once again, generalizations turn out to be wrong – we can only lead a good, happy life by finding the right balance. To determine whether we should try to ignore what others thinks of us, we will first evaluate why we care what others think of us. Then we will determine which forms of caring about other people's opinions are dangerous and which are not. Finally, we will try to find a way to get us on the better side of this relationship.

Is it normal to care what others think?

From our personal lives, we know that we are all concerned with what others think of us, at least, to some extent. We think about the impression that we make, we try to convey a certain image, and we are unhappy when others think of us the wrong way. Scientific research has found evidence that this desire to manage our public image is perfectly natural. Throughout evolution, our chances of survival depended on the image other people had of us. To be a member of a certain group, to receive help from others, and to find a partner, we had to make sure that others considered us valuable. Those of our ancestors who conveyed a positive image had a higher chance to survive and pass on their genes. Over many thousands of generations, this desire has been hard-wired into our genes.

Our ancestors were no tricksters and liars who only survived because they misled others. If our ancestors had failed to manage the image they conveyed, other group members might not have realized their positive qualities, thus abandoning a valuable group member because they failed to recognize their worth. Managing their image was equally helpful to each ancestor and the group they lived in.

We always interact with the image we have of one another. When we perceive someone as trustworthy, we treat them differently than someone we perceive as devious. Our assessments might be wrong, and we might trust people who do not deserve to be trusted, but we can never see other people as they are, only as we perceive them to be. Since this system works both ways, we have a desire that others perceive us positively, that they recognize the qualities we have.

To be concerned about one's public image is perfectly normal. We all are, and anybody claiming that they are not is lying. Do you know someone who is indifferent to what *anybody* thinks of them, including their partner, friends, and parents? Someone who has no problem when everybody thinks of them as an incompetent, immoral, filthy idiot? No mentally healthy person thinks like that.

As a result, any advice to stop caring about other people's opinions is futile – just as futile as saying that the magic solution to losing weight is to not be hungry. Of course we are hungry – it is a healthy feeling that alerts us to vital bodily needs, a feeling that we must allow. We might wish that we could switch it off, but that would create more problems than it would solve. When we try to eliminate feelings that are impossible to eliminate, we inevitably fail. We are ashamed and create false replacements, starting the vicious cycle and making us unhappy.

Self-Help Deception #33: We can ignore others people's opinions of us.

Instead of fighting a battle we are doomed to lose, we are better off accepting our emotional reality and dealing with it effectively. To understand how we can do this, let's take a closer look at why we care what others think of us and which types of negative behavior it can create.

Why are we so concerned with what others think of us?

When self-help books discuss our concern about other people's opinions, they create the impression that this concern has only negative effects. That is not true. Because we care about others' opinions, we can live together in groups and function as a society. If we were indifferent about others, we would be incapable of working in teams and of following a common goal. We could not help each other, we could not feel empathy, and we could not keep a conversation going. Caring about others' opinions is essential to our success as a society and a species.

At the same time, conveying a positive image is essential to achieving our goals. Whether we want to find a partner, have friends, or get a job, whether we want to be respected as a leader, loved as a parent, or valued as a member of society – the image other people have of us decides most of life's important outcomes. To achieve success, we need to add value to other people's lives. Their opinion of us is a direct indicator of our success. Ignoring this indicator means ignoring what it takes to lead a good life. We instinctively know that. We also know that others need help to form an accurate impression of us. Therefore, we want to make sure that they have the impression that we want them to have. This is not inherently wrong.

Self-Help Deception #34: Caring what others think of us has only negative consequences.

While our desire to convey a positive image sometimes leads to negative behavior, that doesn't mean that we should ignore what others think of us. We have to find the middle ground. To understand what this middle ground looks like, let's take a look at what researchers have found about how and why we manage our impression on others.

1. We mostly convey true but selective images about ourselves

When we manage our image, we rarely try to create an image that is completely inaccurate. We merely decide which of the many parts of ourselves we want others to know.

In every situation, there are plenty of different things we could convey about ourselves. We select those that display ourselves the way we want others to think of us. Again, this is not inherently bad. If we did not adapt to each situation, we would constantly display information that is irrelevant to the people we meet. By tailoring the image we want to portray, we guarantee functioning social interactions. Back in my football days, for example, when the other players and I talked to our team doctor, most of us were completely fine; when we talked to our private doctors, we tried to convey a realistic image of our injuries; and when we talked to our girlfriends, we needed immediate care-taking. None of these images was a complete lie, but we chose which part of the wide array of possible images we displayed to whom. We used the image that we hoped would help us get the reaction we wanted but also the image that was best for the situation. Our girlfriends *wanted* to take care of us when we were hurt, our team doctor *wanted* us to play, our private doctors *wanted* to know the truth. Because we cared about the image others had of us, we adapted perfectly to every single situation – a win-win situation for everybody involved.

2. When we lie about ourselves, we mostly use small lies

Sometimes, we lie and convey a wrong image of ourselves, but we mostly use small, harmless lies. When people ask us how we are doing, we may want to avoid a conversation about why we feel bad. So we lie and say we are fine. These small lies help us manage how much information about ourselves we convey to whom, which is a necessary mechanism for handling our social lives. They do no harm, and there is no need to eliminate them.

3. Some people lie more than others

Some people take impression management one step further – they intentionally lie to create a false impression. Psychologists call this behavior *Machiavellianism*. Niccolò Machiavelli was an Italian political philosopher of the 15th century who, in his book *The Prince*, claimed that political leaders should do whatever is necessary to gain and maintain power – they should lie, deceive, and manipulate. To Machiavelli, the end always justified the means. People who lean towards Machiavellianism have adapted Machiavelli's political ideas to their daily lives. As long as they think they can get away with it, Machiavellianists present whatever image they think helps them get what they want.

We are all Machiavellianists but in varying degrees. The key to a happy social life is to keep our Machiavellian tendencies as low as possible. Living our true selves can help us with that. When we do what has intrinsic value to us, we are perfectly content with who we are and what we do – we do not need to convey a more positive image of ourselves, because, in our mind, our real image is the best image we could ever convey. We do what we love, and we love what we do. We can accept others pursuing different paths and having more success, because we do not need to lie to compete with them. We understand that they are running a different race.

4. Sometimes we want to convey a negative image

Most of the time, we are trying to convey a positive image of ourselves. We want others to think of us as friendly, trustworthy, and intelligent people. Still, there are some instances when we intentionally convey a negative image. This happens when we think that a negative image will help us get what we want.

We convey a negative image for various purposes:

- To avoid responsibility. We hope that our boss will assign the task we hate to someone else if he thinks we are incapable of doing it.
- To make others like us. When we think others will be threatened by our intelligence, we play dumb.
- To get others to do what we want. We hope that coming across as highly impatient will get others to do things faster.

Most of the time, these images also are a true part of our personality and communicating them is not inherently negative either.

For the most part, worrying about what other people think of is perfectly natural, it has no negative consequences, and it helps us live together as a society. Only when we take things too far, do we act destructively. We cross this line when we go from choosing which of the many true images of ourselves we display to creating a false image and manipulating people. It is perfectly natural to be proud of who we are and to want others to recognize our positive qualities and achievements, but we create problems when we want to be recognized for qualities we do not have or things we did not achieve. Living our true selves helps us to stay on the better side of this equation.

While it is perfectly normal to care what others think of us and to manage the image we convey, there are two downsides to our desire to convey a certain image:

- It causes social anxiety, and
- It causes negative behavior that hurts us and others.

Let's take a closer look at these two downsides, and find out how we can avoid them.

How can we avoid social anxiety?

We all know how social anxiety feels. On job interviews and dates, when we meet new people, and when we have to give a speech, we want to make a good impression. Often, we are unsure that we can, so we get anxious. The more we want to make a good impression and the less we think we can pull it off, the more anxious we get.

In many ways, social anxiety is a helpful feeling. It helps us to understand when it is important to make a good impression. When we feel anxious because of a job interview, we prepare and dress better than we would for an evening with our friends. Without social anxiety, we might go to a job interview in sweatpants, knowing nothing about the company.

Social anxiety can, however, also become a problem. When we feel anxious, we often become quiet and withdraw from a situation. While it makes sense to rather say nothing than say what we think will cause others to think badly of us, our silence can cause exactly what we are trying to avoid. We know this, and get more anxious and quiet. In the worst case, we find ourselves starting a circle of anxiety that makes us withdraw more and more.

To fix this situation, self-help literature often gives tips on how to feel better about ourselves and how to raise our self-esteem. As we have seen, these tips fail to improve our quality of life – inflated self-esteem is harmful. Advice to convey a better image than we have of ourselves is a page out of Machiavelli's book: to get what you want, lie about yourself.

We can fight social anxiety more effectively by creating better lives. As we do what has intrinsic value to us, our lives get closer to what we consider a good life. We can convey a better yet still realistic image. Because we are satisfied and content with who we are, because we no longer feel inferior or ashamed, we are more confident that we can convey the image we desire and feel less socially anxious – we have eliminated the reason for our social anxiety, not just changed our way of thinking.

Additionally, living our true selves automatically shifts our focus in a way that psychologists discovered to be the best way to overcome our fears and anxieties. According to *acceptance and commitment therapy (ACT)*,[5] fighting our fears head on by telling ourselves that there is no need to be afraid is futile and intensifies our fear. Being constantly reminded that our fears are irrational causes us to find explanations for why we are afraid anyway. We focus on the events that created the fear and start to see ourselves as inherently broken – an unhealthy attitude that worsens the problem and creates shame and false replacements. Instead, ACT ignores the question why we are afraid of something and tries to attach what we are afraid of to the values we are passionate about. When we understand why something is important to us, so says the theory, we can act despite our fear and overcome it.

Before ACT, psychologists tried to treat a fear of flying by listing arguments why flying is safe and why a fear of flying is irrational. This approach often ended in a tug of war between the psychologists' arguments and the patients' fears, thereby reinforcing those fears. With ACT, psychologists end this tug of war by dropping the rope. Instead of focusing on the patient's fear, psychologists appeal to the patient's dreams and passions. They show the patient how flying can help them do what they are passionate about.

To eliminate false replacements, ACT reminds the patients of their true selves. By living our true selves, we accomplish the same thing but without the need for expensive therapy. Much like ACT, our true selves are indifferent to why we are afraid of something or how unfortunate

---

[5] For further information on ACT, I recommend you read one of the books by Steven Hayes, the founding father of ACT. A good starting point should be: Hayes, Steven C.; Kirk D. Strosahl: *A Practical Guide to Acceptance and Commitment Therapy.*

circumstances forced us to develop this fear. Our true selves are result-orientated, they want to contribute to something. If anxiety attempts to stop us from contributing, our true selves try to work around the anxiety. They will not accept it as an insurmountable obstacle. This solves the problem in the same way as ACT does, and it stops new anxieties from developing.

Neither ACT nor living our true selves will be able to eliminate our fears, but they help us to use our passion to outweigh our fears and take the first step. These first steps help us to understand that what we were afraid of might be less dangerous than we expected while simultaneously allowing us a taste of the rewards that we could reap if we overcome our fears. We gradually reduce our fear and eventually overcome it completely.

The great advantage of this approach is that we do not have to eliminate our fear before we can get moving, we can start right away. Our true selves are the first step to overcoming any fear.

How does controlling our image cause destructive behaviors?

Worrying about what others think of us can sometimes cause destructive behavior. Teenagers often engage in dangerous behaviors to impress others – they jump from the roof into a faraway pool, they drive recklessly, or they drink too much. As adults, we consider ourselves to be above this type of behavior, but we frequently do the same thing.

- A large share of all deaths due to skin cancer are the result of endless sunbathing because we want to be pretty.
- We waste a big part of our money on products and surgeries that promise everlasting youth because we want others to think of us as beautiful.
- Eating disorders are largely the result of us wanting to have others consider us skinny.

Similarly, we often base big life decisions on the image we want to convey to others:

- We work endless hours in jobs we hate, only to buy things to impress our neighbors.
- We neglect our families and our health to be what others want us to be.
- We go to social activities we despise because we think we are expected to.
- We choose partners and spouses to impress others with them.
- When we need help, crutches, or other types of assistance, we reject them because we are afraid of appearing needy.

These types of behavior are destructive. We think that our true life situation is something we need to hide, something to be ashamed of – a thought that we will cope with by creating false replacements. For many of us, every single step we take is motivated by how others want us to be. When these decisions fail to create happiness, this is no surprise – creating happiness was not part of our decision. As a result, we often neglect the things that could make us happy for what could impress others. We do what has no intrinsic value to us and become unhappy.

We can avoid this trap by being aware of it. Knowing that our desire to convey a positive image is natural but that we should stop it from distracting us from what has intrinsic value to us helps us to manage our behavior and invest our effort where we need it most. We can pursue what has intrinsic value and eliminate most of the rest.

In psychological terms, people who deny their feelings to convey an image are considered narcissists. Knowing this distinction can help us to take our feelings and passions more seriously. It is perfectly okay to choose which part of us we convey to whom, but once we start neglecting who we are to convey a certain image, we make our lives worse.

How your friends can make you unhappy

When it comes to our friends and partners, our desire to have others think well of us can cause us to hold onto false replacements that we would otherwise abandon. Since we all want our friends to have something in common with us, we have two options when we choose friends:

1. We can choose friends based on false replacements.
2. We can choose friends based on our true selves.

Unfortunately, many of us make the mistake to choose friends based on a false replacement. We choose friends to drink with, to shop with, or to smoke with, and friends that also deal with their insecurities by sexual conquest, materialism, minimalism, or working too much. In these situations, giving up the shared false replacement would mean to destroy the common ground the relationships are built on – a scary thought that threatens all our essential needs. We are left with two possibilities:

1. We can do what most of our friends will consider wrong and experience rejection and unhappiness.
2. We can keep doing what has no intrinsic value to us and also experience unhappiness.

The first option can help us lead better lives. While both alternatives create unhappiness, the unhappiness of losing friends will fade, as we saw in chapter 2 ("What makes us happy?"). We will find new friends, and we still have other things left that can make us happy. The unhappiness of doing what has no intrinsic value to us, however, is everlasting. Nonetheless, because we are concerned with what others think of us, we often choose the second option and keep the common false replacement alive.

To avoid having to decide between two negatives, we can choose friends and partners that share a part of our true selves. A common passion makes our relationship more intrinsically rewarding and stable, thereby contributing to our happiness.

Conclusion

1. Being concerned about other people's opinions is perfectly normal and healthy – there's no need to fight it.
2. Not caring about others' opinions creates more problems than it solves. When we try to do what we can't do – ignoring others' opinions – we inevitably fail. We feel shame and create false replacements. It is better to accept that we care and manage our care well.
3. Our desire to convey a positive image is tied to problems such as Machiavellianism and social anxiety. First and foremost, however, these problems are the result of bad life decisions, not the result of our desire to convey a positive image.
4. We can solve the problems related to conveying a positive image by leading better lives, by doing what has intrinsic value to us. Then we will be satisfied with the image we naturally convey and can refrain from manipulating it.

Further reading

Erving Goffman: The Presentation of Self in Everyday life.

An introduction to how we manage our public image based on scientific research, comparing our daily lives to actors in a theatrical play – insightful and amusing.

Mark Leary: Self-presentation. Impression Management and Interpersonal Behavior.

An analysis of why we care what others think of us, how this concern influences our behavior, and how we can stop our desire for self-presentation from making our lives worse.

Chapter 15

How to know what to believe

"I like the scientific spirit – the holding off, the being sure but not too sure, the willingness to surrender ideas when the evidence is against them: this is ultimately fine – it always keeps the way beyond open – always gives life, thought, affection, the whole man, a chance to try over again after a mistake – after a wrong guess."

WALT WHITMAN

For more than 2,000 years, doctors believed that many illnesses were the result of excess blood in the body. As a treatment, these doctors cut open their patients' veins and let the blood run out. The procedure was repeated for months. When a patient had so little blood left that it was no longer coming out on its own, the doctors put a tube with heated air over the wound. The air cooled, created a vacuum, and pulled out even more blood. Then they put leeches on the patient's veins to suck out the last drops of blood left in the body. Unsurprisingly, bloodletting, as the procedure was called, failed to improve the patients' chances of healing. In fact, many patients died. Doctors, who often performed hundreds of bloodlettings, knew this. Yet they kept using the method until the 19th century. It was not until we discovered new, better methods that we discarded this old, obviously wrong theory.

Did we learn from our mistake? No. In the 20th century, lobotomies became common practice. In an attempt to cure mental illnesses, psychiatrists destroyed a part of their patients' brains with an ice pick. While the treatment left patients incapacitated for life or killed them, it was not until the late 1950s when new treatments became available, and the use of lobotomies started to decline. These examples show an ever recurring error of human thinking: we do not discard an idea when it is proven wrong, we only discard an idea when there's a better alternative available.

Sometimes, we even believe in wrong ideas if there's a better theory available. Many people still try to lose weight by avoiding fat, sugar, gluten, or salt, even though we know with absolute certainty that weight loss is a matter of burning more calories than we consume. We often believe in ideas that are clearly wrong, even though there are better alternatives available. These theories inevitably set us up for failure and shame and create false replacements. Masked as political ideologies, such ideas have killed millions of people.

If these lies have such negative consequences, then why do we believe in them so desperately? And how can we avoid this process? Now that we have eliminated the most notorious self-help deceptions, how can we avoid falling for similarly destructive ideas again?

Why do we believe in something?

To understand why we believe in lies so willingly, let's go back to our first example of bloodletting. Imagine you are sick. The doctor tells you that there's nothing he can do for you. How do you feel? Powerless? Uncertain? Insignificant? Scared? However you would describe it, you would probably feel pretty bad. What if another doctor would offer you an unproven treatment that, as he claims, might help you? If you are like most of us, this glimpse of hope will make you feel less powerless, less uncertain, and less bad. That is why most of us would accept it. We do what helps us feel best, not what is best for us. That is a huge difference, and that is why bloodletting and lobotomy were accepted treatments: they helped us satisfy our essential needs:

- Certainty („This will help"),
- Possibility („Things will be better soon"),
- Significance ("You made the right decision by choosing me"), and
- Love ("You are so smart that you came to me").

When doctors admit that they are unable to help us, they fail to satisfy any of these needs.

That's why we do not only need a better theory available to discard a wrong theory; we need a better theory that can satisfy our basic needs. Intuitively, we would rather have a wrong answer than no answer at all or an answer that feels worse – we use the wrong answer as a false replacement. This false replacement can get us into great danger. Many people reject proven medical treatments for a well-sounding lie, which can potentially kill them.

Believing lies in our private lives

Knowingly believing in lies extends beyond medicine. Many of us are constantly searching for the one idea that can solve all our problems or can effortlessly create a perfect society. Since reality is always more complicated, our daily lives are filled with the same error of thought:

- How long do we stay in an unhappy relationship? Until we see a chance for a better relationship.
- How long do we believe that a supernatural being caused something? Until we find a scientific explanation.

- How long do we believe that the country we are born in is the greatest and best country in the world? Until we see enough of the world to know better.
- How long do we believe that there is a simple, quick fix to political issues? Until we tried the quick fix and know that it doesn't work.

It would be better to know these facts in advance. It would help us make better decisions and lead better lives. When we are in an unhappy relationship, it would help to know that we are better off ending the relationship right now. When we discuss the big bang, it would speed up human progress to leave supernatural powers out of it. Understanding the truth always helps us lead better lives. When we stop clinging to wrong ideas, we free ourselves to allow true and better things to come into our lives. That might feel a little scary at first, but in the long run, it will pay off a thousand-fold. Therefore, it is important to understand how our minds can be tricked into believing lies, how some people try to take advantage of our predispositions, and how we can control the accuracy of our beliefs.

Self-Help Deception #35: When we believe in something we should pursue it without questioning why we believe it.

What can we do to avoid believing in lies?

Even when we understand why we believe in lies, it is hard to avoid their effects every time. Still, there are a few things we can do to make sure we can overcome wrong ideas:

- We can constantly question our beliefs. Do we believe something because there is solid evidence or because it makes us feel better? We must never believe anything simply because it makes us feel good.
- When the facts disprove our beliefs, we must discard the beliefs. We can admit we were wrong. Any belief that is not supported by evidence is a lie and will make our lives worse.
- If we have no replacement theory in place, we must learn to accept the limits of our knowledge. It is better to have no answer than to believe in a wrong answer.

How to avoid destructive ideologies

In our modern world, it becomes increasingly important to question everything we believe in. From 1950 to 2000, the number of scientists worldwide rose from 10 million to 100 million. This dramatic increase in scientific capacity has led to a similarly dramatic increase in knowledge. As a result, the amount of things we truly understand is decreasing rapidly. My dad, who was born in 1954, was still able to understand and fix the hardware of the first computers he owned. Nowadays, hardly anybody knows how a smartphone works. Most electronic devices have become a black box we fail to understand. Similarly, most people fail to grasp the complexity of international conflicts, of financial and economic decisions, and of many other aspects of life. That is dangerous. When we are surrounded by black boxes, we have to believe what other people tell us about them. This increases the risk of somebody taking advantage of us and opens the door for propaganda and misinformation.

So what can we do? We can't know everything, and we can't simply believe what others tell us. We need a system to evaluate whether what someone is telling us makes sense or not, a system that works without having a lot of information about the topic in question.

We can do this by evaluating an argument's style of reasoning. Liars, agitators, and other people who want to use our lack of information for their own benefit reveal themselves by arguing in a certain way. When we understand this way, we can eliminate most ways of thinking about the world from the start. Most people who spread lies, intentionally or unintentionally, argue by using three elements of faulty logic in their argumentation:

- Feeling-based truth,
- Argument from ignorance,
- Confirmation bias.

We already talked about the confirmation bias, but let's take a closer look at the first two elements:

Feelings determine the truth

On September 11, 2001, I was on a school trip to Paris, France. We visited the Eiffel Tower and had a normal day. In the late afternoon, after we had returned to our hostel, we saw the World Trade Center collapse live on TV. We were shocked. Nobody could believe what they were seeing. Strangely enough, though, this disbelief quickly changed into a strange sense of certainty. Within minutes, everybody had pieced together his own theory of what had happened. Now the arguing started. Even though none of us knew anything, we all felt completely sure of our theories. A few days later, when the first shock had passed, we were still arguing. With every new piece of information, we all believed that it proved our theories.

In the months after the attack, I often wondered what drove us to act so ridiculously. None of us knew what we were talking about, but that did little to stop us from passionately asserting our opinions. While the logical approach would have been to agree that we were all clueless and wait for further developments, we were incapable of acting logically.

In many ways, what happened with my school class after 9/11 resembles the challenges of dealing with complex problems. Often, the truth is unsettling and seemingly random. Equipped with an emotional system that has been evolutionary trained to survive in small groups in the wild under much easier to grasp circumstances, we often have trouble grasping what is happening in our modern, more complex and less certain world. Therefore, we desperately need to come up with an explanation. Similar to what happened with bloodletting and lobotomies, our desire for an explanation is driven by our four basic needs. When we are unable to explain what is happening, we fail to fulfill those needs:

- We are unsure of what is happening – we lack certainty.
- We know that we can hardly make a good decision – we lack a sense of possibility.
- We realize that we are but a small piece in a big world which can be wiped out immediately – we lack significance.
- We feel that there are big forces at work that are indifferent to our needs – we lack love/connection.

When we come up with a theory to explain the world despite a complete lack of information, we can satisfy all these needs.

- We know what's happening – we feel certainty.
- We know what to do – we feel possibility.
- We think that we recognized the hidden truth – we feel significant.
- We feel smarter than everybody else – we feel love for ourselves.

From an evolutionary standpoint, this mechanism makes a lot of sense. It helped us make quick decisions in dangerous situations. When a predator was attacking, we needed to be decisive. Those humans who immediately started running in any direction had, at least, some chance to survive, even if they knew little about what lay in this direction. Weighing all possible alternatives would have allowed the predator to come closer – a potentially deadly delay. Being absolutely convinced we made the right decision increased the chances for survival. Most likely, decisiveness cost as many human lives as it saved, but our ancestors who ran into dead ends or into other predators never procreated either. We are the descendants of humans that survived because they made quick decisions based on limited information. Through thousands of generations, this mechanism was ingrained into our brains. Today, it still controls our behavior. We are emotionally unable to accept that we have no knowledge of something. Our evolution-shaped instincts tell us that not having a theory of how to deal with an issue could be dangerous – in an evolutionary sense; any theory is better than no theory. Our egos want to have a fixed set of rules by which they can interpret any situation and decide how to resolve the inherent conflict between the id and the super-ego. Without this set of rules, our egos are paralyzed.

In our modern times, we face far more complicated decisions than our ancestors. They often had only two options: to flee or to attack, to run left or right. Even if they had no information to base their decision on, they had a fifty-fifty chance of getting it right. Nowadays, we can regularly choose from thousands of alternatives, dramatically reducing the odds of making a good decision based on limited information. Demagogues use this lack of certainty to present us with simple theories that we can understand and that can satisfy our needs. 9/11 truthers, communists, racists, etc. all present a simple answer to a complex problem – they say, "It's their fault, let's eliminate them and everything will be fine."

This reasoning works because it appeals to our shame. Accepting the premise that we can free ourselves from shame if we fight against the villain the destructive ideology proclaims can even make us cross the threshold to harm other people. Ideologies that have the potential to create violence validate the shame we feel and promise to be the relief for this shame, thereby positioning themselves as false replacements.

- Most Germans were ashamed of having accepted the repressive peace treaty of Versailles after World War I. Adolf Hitler promised to avenge this shame, which brought large parts of the society on his side and was a main reason for the attacks on France, England, and Russia.

- Many of us feel shame for certain things we have done. By declaring mankind inherently sinful and in need of salvation, religions appeal to the shame in us and create faithful followers, which is why some people are willing to go to war over religious matters.

- Subconsciously, many workers feel ashamed for being powerless before their employers. Communism promises to turn this relationship on its head. The prospect of a relief from shame can trick workers into supporting the dispossession of people, even though they would never allow themselves, their family, or the friends to be dispossessed.

- Racism and nationalism are so attractive to many because they imply that our values and beliefs are better than any other values and beliefs, promising to relieve us from the shame we feel about not being a perfect person. These ideas imply that we do not have to be ashamed of our actions because we will always be better than people of a different skin color – a promise that can trick us into supporting violence.

By appealing to our feelings and our shame, destructive ideas can trick us into believing the worst kind of lies. In the process, we will hurt ourselves and others.

Argument from ignorance

After simplifying the problem and creating an easy villain, destructive ideologies constitute an argument from ignorance to explain their theory. Argument from ignorance means saying "I do not know what that is, and, therefore, it must be X." We all know arguments from ignorance from our daily lives:

- When some people see an object in the sky that they fail to understand, they conclude that it must be a spaceship from a different planet. This might be the least likely of all possible explanations, but as long as it satisfies our needs, we believe it.

- When some people see an unbelievable tragedy such as the 9/11 attacks, they conclude that this must be the result of a government conspiracy with hundreds of thousands of people involved. This explanation is highly unlikely, but it satisfies our needs for certainty and significance more than accepting that a handful of terrorists successfully attacked the United States.

- When some people hear that millions of people touched a stone and three of them felt better, they conclude that they have witnessed a miracle. This explanation is much more unlikely than accepting that if millions of people touched anything, a few of them are bound to feel better, but believing in miracles from a higher power helps us satisfy our needs.

Destructive ideologies employ the same mechanism. Much like every flying object a UFO believer fails to understand automatically becomes an alien spacecraft, every problem in our society becomes the fault of the ideology's proclaimed villain. Whatever the villain does, they only prove the ideology's preconceived ideas – the ideology has become invincible. Over time, the conflict will be reinforced and strengthened, until it results in oppression, persecution, and violence.

- As studies have shown, men who violently attack gay people are more aroused by gay porn than the average male. Their anti-gay ideology is a false replacement to deal with the shame they feel for their own homosexual tendencies. For homosexuals, it is hard to do anything against these prejudices. Whatever they do, their actions are seen as proof of the preconceived ideology.

- Some religious people fight against scientifically proven theories such as evolution and try to stop homosexuals from getting married. Neither of these ideas presents any threat to them, but since these ideas question the ideology that they use as a false replacement to deal with their shame, these people invest much time and effort into stopping progress and ruling other people's lives. They discard any reasonable explanation of scientific discoveries as propaganda and evoke a dangerous anti-intellectualism – their ideology has become invincible.

- When some people hear of a problem in our society but fail to grasp the complex socio-economic factors that caused it, they are quick to blame it on their ideologies standard villain. "Unemployment has gone up? Must be the fault of the capitalists, the Jews, the foreign workers, the media, the infidels, the Muslims, etc."

None of these ideologies present any helpful solutions to the actual problem. They are a way of trying to make ourselves feel better while intensifying the problem, inventing new problems, and making ourselves feel worse – they are destructive. To be happy, we must learn to recognize destructive ideologies and avoid them.

We are all susceptible to destructive ideologies

While it is easy to recognize false replacements in others, we must avoid falling for a self-serving bias and overestimating the purity of our motives. To be susceptible to dangerous ideas, we must fulfill two criteria:

1. We must feel shame.
2. We must lack information.

While it is easy to see that we are all ashamed of some things we've done or some things about ourselves, most people underestimate how little information they have in almost all aspects of their lives, thereby overestimating the quality of their beliefs.

In many ways, our decision-making process compares to the life of a farm animal. Based on all the information a farm animal has, it must conclude that humans are kind – they provide it with food and shelter, they take care of it when it is sick. There's not a single reason to discard this belief – until the animal is slaughtered and eaten. With the limited information it has, the animal can't possibly see this coming – but it would greatly benefit if it could. Every day that the animal decides to stay on the farm, it is making a bad decision. Tragically, it is incapable of knowing its mistake until it is too late. The only way for any animal to find out whether it is a good idea to live with humans is to wait until it dies. If it dies from a natural cause, it was a pet. If it gets slaughtered, it was a farm animal.

In many ways, our decision-making process with limited information resembles the life of a farm animal. Often, years pass between the day we make a decision and the day we find out whether it was right or wrong. During the entire time, we face a dilemma. We still have time to correct our decision, but we are unsure about whether we should. Equipped with a mind that is evolutionarily trained to make short-term decisions with quick feedback, we lack a good tool to make decisions over decades. Every day smokers decide to keep smoking; they are very likely making a decision that will kill them eventually – but they'll only know that for sure when it happens. There is a chance that they will die from a different cause and that smoking will not shorten their lives after all. This way of thinking might sound absurd, but it gives most smokers a much-needed excuse.

Similarly, when we believe that our religion will save us from eternal damnation, that our fight against a certain group of people is necessary to save society, or that harming someone will create a better world, we can only realize that we were wrong by completing our mission. Until then, we might doubt the path that we are on, but we can never be sure. There is always a chance that it might be the right path. Much like a smoker, this possibility keeps us going:

- Even if we despise violence, we might accept hurting others, because we are not sure that it is wrong "in this rare case."
- We might support the restriction of basic human rights, either for all of us or a group of people. We will say that we dislike the idea, but that it might be justified "in this extreme situation."
- Even if we know that we lack the necessary skills to succeed, we hope that our positivity will create a miracle "this one time."

Step by step, this process can cause us to surrender our morals, our freedom, and the values that are dearest to us. After World War II, many Germans told American troops that they rejected Hitler's general hatred of the Jews, but that he was justified to persecute them "in this rare case." A perfect example of the process we laid out above.

In our modern world, our brains face a dilemma. Without any quality information, our ego is often at a loss. The id, on the other hand, wants its needs satisfied immediately. Overwhelmed by the id and with the super-ego undecided, the ego has to go for the only sure indication it has. The immediate, concrete reward has triumphed over the abstract, distant reward. Luckily, there's one big difference between farm animals and humans – we have the power to anticipate future events. We can understand complex mechanisms and transfer what happened to other members of our species to ourselves. If we were in the position of a farm animal, seeing other animals disappear and be replaced by the day, we could easily conclude that we, too, will someday disappear and that it may be better not to wait for that day. Due to the lack of certain information, however, our egos are incapable of making this decision, neglecting the mental advantage we have over animals.

We can fight this disadvantage by supporting our ego's ability to create certain predictions – by educating ourselves. Fittingly, education is the most effective way to avoid an argument from ignorance. Regarding smoking, this is easy. There is plenty of information out there to counter the claims that smoking is a fun, adventurous sign of freedom and not at all dangerous –

easily enough information to make a good decision once we eliminated our false replacements. In other situations, the necessary information is more difficult to obtain, or events occur only rarely and with intervals of years in between. These situations are trickier but often more important – politics, big life decisions, and whether or not we should believe in self-help books.

How to not become a Nazi

Believing in lies on a small scale can only hurt us. While self-inflicted pain is tragic, it is even more tragic when our false replacements hurt others. Demagogues know how limited information makes us manipulable. They spread their ideas in a way that appeals to our needs. In all cases, the message is the same:

1. All problems in your life and society are someone else's fault.

By putting all blame on one group, either a minority or a group outside the country, destructive ideologies acquit all other people of any responsibility for problems in their lives and society. Since we all face some level of self-doubt, this relieves us from our shame. We know that it is not our fault, and we have found certainty.

2. When this one group is gone, everything will be better.

When destructive ideologies promise to free us from the people who allegedly harm us or society, they imply that our lives will be better when this one group is gone or disempowered. Imagining how good our lives will be with all our problems solved is a message that appeals to many. Accepting the belief that someone else is to blame for our problems and having someone promise to get these people out of our way creates the feeling of possibility that we've been missing for so long.

3. You are a member of a big group that will always stand together.

Hitler called it the "Volksgemeinschaft" (ethnic community), communists call it the proletariat, other ideologies call it believers vs. infidels, wolves vs. sheep, or go-getters vs. underachievers. All terms are meant to create a feeling of love and connection towards a fictional concept without any real-life implications. Being a member of a special group, even if it is entirely made-up, gives us a feeling of love/connection. Many of us feel a lack of love/connection in our daily lives and welcome the thought of having everyone around us support us to fill this void.

4. You are something special

As we grow up, most of us have to realize that we are average. Whatever we are good at – there's someone who's better. When we fail to realize our dreams, we feel a lack of significance. Believing that we are something special because we belong to a certain group can fill this void.

How to avoid destructive lies

Any attempt to use a void in our four essential needs to make us believe in a lie can be preempted by naturally fulfilling our needs. When we are fulfilled, happy, and pursue intrinsic goals, we are fine without an ideology that can work as a false replacement. Nonetheless, it can sometimes be hard to know what to believe. In those cases, there are four rules that can help us distinguish constructive ideas from destructive ideas – in politics, life, self-help and all other cases.

When faced with an idea or ideology that goes beyond our understanding, we first have to admit that we are unsure whether the idea or ideology is true. Then, we can use these four rules that any worthwhile theory must fulfill to find out whether the theory is destructive or not.

1. We are all humans – any division into groups is wrong.

Regardless of whether an ideology wants to divide us by skin color, social status, religion, land of birth, sexual orientation, age, political belief or anything else – any division is wrong. We are all humans, and any worthwhile philosophy of life will point out our similarities, not our differences. As we can see in chapter 13 ("How to evaluate ourselves reasonably"), we tend to overvalue anything that is associated with us, including our values. As soon as we start dividing the world into *us* and *them*, we inevitably overvalue what is associated with *us* and devalue what is associated with *them* – psychologists call this the *in-group/out-group bias*. Since both groups go through a similar process, we have created two rival groups, each convinced of its superiority and full of resentment towards the other – we have sown the seed for conflict, war, and suffering. To avoid this dangerous process, we have to remain united as human beings.

2. Nobody is more or less special than anybody else.

While we are all different, nobody is better than anybody else, nobody deserves preferential treatment, and nobody must be fought. Only those who hurt others, or damage or steal other people's property must be stopped from repeating their infractions – nothing else. There is no chosen group, nobody has found the truth, and nobody has any secrets to unveil.

3. We are individuals, not members of a predefined group.

There is no Volksgemeinschaft and no other form of predefined group that we inherently belong to. We are humans and outside of our families, we equally belong to any human group in the world. We can only lead good, happy lives if we individually find our place in this world, our ideal group, and gain its acceptance by contributing to the group's success.

Similarly, one person's actions are not reflective of any group they associate with. Just because one person steals, not all of his colleagues are thieves, too. (Unless they were involved in the crime, of course.)

4. There is no need to be ashamed of who we are

Some ideologies tell us that we are inherently bad or sinful and need this ideology to be saved. This is a trick. The ideology creates shame and the need for a false replacement in us and then positions itself as this false replacement – the perfect situation for any ideology to keep us forever dependent on it. Sometimes, ideologies adapt this trick consciously; sometimes it is the result of an accidental process that keeps the ideology alive for thousands of years. Either way, this type of story is a lie.

These four rules can help us distinguish worthwhile ideas from destructive lies. Any idea that violates these rules is a false replacement. Someone else wants to use our lack of knowledge to their advantage or has fallen for a destructive ideology themselves. In any decision, if there is more than one idea left that abides by all these rules, we can find the best idea available by choosing the idea that has the most factual proof, that seeks out disconfirming evidence, and that can stand without requiring us to accept anything on authority. Nonetheless, we should always be open for a better idea to come along.

Self-help violates all of these rules. Self-help divides the world into us, the go-getters who know how to live the right way, and them, the people with limiting beliefs, implying that we are better than them and more deserving of happiness, success, and all other good things. This reasoning inevitably creates a lack of compassion for those who are less fortunate than we are and suggests that the world would be a better place if everyone followed our way.

Why we profit most by avoiding lies

When we avoid false replacements packaged as ideologies, the potential victims of these ideologies are not the only people who profit – first and foremost, we profit ourselves. As soon as we subscribe to a false ideology, we start building our lives on a lie, setting ourselves up for certain and repeated failure. Regardless of whether this false replacement comes packaged as an ideology, an idea, or a self-help book, it tricks us into pursuing what we can never achieve. Sooner or later, the inevitable disappointment generated by such a lie will cause shame in us and make us create more false replacements. This happens when we believe in the dominant self-help mentality, in conspiracy theories, or in political lies such as socialism, nationalism, or fascism – we pursue what we can never achieve, and when we fail, we create false replacements that make our lives worse.

Conclusion

1. In our modern, complex world, there is little we know for certain.
2. Uncertain information causes bad decisions. We can make better decisions by educating ourselves.
3. We can distinguish worthwhile ideas, theories, and ideologies from lies packaged as false replacements by analyzing how an ideology tries to appeal to us. Ideologies that use an emotional approach, positioning themselves as potential false replacements, are destructive. In a worthwhile ideology, there is no division, no generalization, nobody is more special than anybody else, and nobody is inherently bad.

Further reading

Karl Popper: The Open Society and its Enemies.
Karl Popper's answer to Nazism, communism, and totalitarian regimes in general, *The Open Society and its Enemies* is probably the best book ever written to show why totalitarian ideas are dangerous and should be avoided. One of the most important books of our time.

Henri Tajfel: Experiments in intergroup discrimination, Scientific American 223, 96-102.
An article about experiments that show that we prefer members of our group over members of other groups, even if we know nothing about them.

Michael Shermer: The Believing Brain: From Spiritual Faiths to Political Convictions - How We Construct Beliefs and Reinforce Them as Truths.
American psychologist Michael Shermer shares 30 years of research on how we create our beliefs and reinforce them as the truth. A great book for anyone who want to avoid being tricked into supporting discrimination, suppression, and hatred against people who disagree with us.

Sigmund Freud: Group Psychology and the Analysis of the Ego.
Freud's take on mass psychology agrees with the premise that any division into groups will inevitably lead to a devaluation of the other group.

Chapter 16

Does success leave clues?

When I started my first blog, I tried to find out how I could make people find me on Google. Many of the articles I read about techniques to generate traffic were written by successful bloggers who, as they said, wanted to share the secret of their success. Most of those articles read more or less like this:

- I have no idea how search engine optimization works.
- I simply published a few posts, and people started streaming in.
- Why? Well, apparently, I'm the best content creator in history.

Naive as I was, I even invested $20 in a book by a successful blogger that essentially said, "Create good content and everything else will magically fall into place. It worked for me, and I can't think of any reason why it shouldn't work for everyone."

I knew this was nonsense. It reminded me of attractive people who refuse to accept that their good looks make social interactions easier. Since they need to explain why they are getting treated so much better, they convince themselves that they have a special character and are much more likable than everybody else. What they are missing, of course, is the elephant in the room: when you are good-looking, people are nicer to you.

Many successful bloggers are also missing the elephant in the room: a blog becomes successful by ranking high in Google. Google's search algorithm is a complex, top secret, and ever changing system. While there are some things bloggers can do to destroy their ranking, the number one reason for ranking high in a system that nobody understands is luck. Of course, good, helpful content is essential to making readers come back and share the articles, and every successful blogger writes good content, but if nobody can find a blogger's great content, success will elude them. Good content is insufficient to guarantee success. Of the thousands of websites that are perfectly optimized, Google ranks only ten on page 1. So why does Google choose perfect site A over perfect site B? Nobody knows. While the owner of site A will think of a million good reasons why his site was sure to rank high, all of them are illusions. To make sense of the world, our brains are looking for patterns that they understand and can interpret, even if there is only randomness. Mistaking these patterns for clues to success can lead to dangerous misconceptions. Self-help often follows a similar approach, claiming to have analyzed a long list of successful people and to have found the common reason for their success.

Success leaves clues, but...

When we compare successful people in any genre, we will always find some consensus. All successful bloggers will tell us that content is king, all successful actors will tell us that we should quit our jobs and go all-in on our acting career, all successful rock stars will tell us to keep touring until we get our big break. That is a misconception. The fact that everybody who succeeded did the same thing does *not* mean that everybody who did the same thing succeeded. There are millions of bloggers who create great, helpful content for blogs that nobody reads. There are thousands of talented actors who never get a role and thousands of good bands that play in empty bars. These failures can teach us as much about success as the success stories. When we try to find out how to succeed at something, we must also study the failures, especially those failures who were every bit as good as the successes. Most of the time, what separated the failures from the successes is luck.

Imagine we start a coin flip tournament with 1,000 people. After one flip, 500 people will have correctly predicted whether their coin will show heads or tails. We let these 500 flip again. After the next flip, there will be 250 players left, then 125, then 63, and so on. After about ten flips, there will be one player left. If our tournament paid a lot of prize money, the lucky winner would become rich. Now everybody would want to know the secret to his success, and he would write a book. He would talk about how to flip the coin the right way, what to think about when flipping the coin, and lots of other superstitious nonsense. The fact that one person thinks that these things helped them succeed is insufficient to help us or anybody else copy their success. When we analyze a person's success, we should take our clues from a non-emotional, scientific evaluation, not from what a successful person thinks caused their success – 99 percent of them have no clue.

In his book *Outliers*, Malcolm Gladwell followed exactly this approach. He analyzed successful people on all aspects of life and tried to find out what separated them from the many unsuccessful people. His result? All of them, from The Beatles and Bill Gates to Robert Oppenheimer and Steve Jobs, essentially were very, very lucky. They were born at just the right time into just the right circumstances. A few years later or earlier, a different town, or one lucky meeting less, and they would have failed. While they made good use of this perfect situation, they were unaware of its existence until they were halfway through their journey. In every success story, luck plays a huge role – and that is the most fundamental fact we know about great success.

Self-Help Deception #36: There is a blueprint we can follow for success.

Should we even try to be successful?

If success is mostly the result of luck, should we all stop trying to be successful? Well, no. Success does leave clues. But those clues are not what successful people say caused their success. Those clues are chaotic, unpredictable accumulations of circumstances. To be as wildly successful as Steve Jobs, The Beatles, or Bill Gates, we have to encounter a similar string of lucky events – but it is impossible to force good circumstances by doing what previous successes did. We can't even tell whether we are in a good situation or not – of all the people who believed that they found exactly what the world needs, only a few succeeded.

In many ways, trying to be successful resembles trying to find a good partner. Most of the people we meet will either be incompatible with us or turn us down. But that that doesn't mean that we should stop trying. There's too much at stake, and there's always the chance for success the next time. We should, however, refrain from hoping for every person we meet to be our savior. The same applies to trying to be successful at something. We can improve our chances by getting ourselves in situations where good things can happen – by starting that blog, by writing that book, by opening that business. In our modern world, one social share by the right person can lead to great success. When we care about something, we have to try to use this chance in our favor. At the same time, there is no reason to put all our eggs in one basket – it is impossible to force luck. Even if we do everything right, things might not work out for reasons beyond our influence. That is important to know because it helps us deduce rules for how to be as successful as possible:

1. Compare how people tried to be successful at something and try to find patterns.
2. Most of the time, you will find that part of these people failed because they made bad decisions. Avoid making the same bad decisions.
3. Find out what the successes did, and do the same thing.
4. Be realistic about your chances of success. A major part of the failures did exactly what the successes did. Their failure can be attributed to bad luck and unpredictable circumstances. By copying the same approach, you will probably fail, too.
5. Try new ideas as low-cost as possible before you invest big. It's better to try many low-cost ideas than one high-cost idea. This increases your odds of creating one idea at the right time and the right place.
6. Never put all your eggs in one basket. Always have a plan B. The whole talk of "Plan B only distracts from plan A" is nonsense spread by people who had very, very good luck.
7. If our success largely depends on chance, even the most successful people are not inherently better or more deserving than others. Other people did an equally great job; they just had worse luck. Should you or I ever be

lucky enough to experience great success, this is a good reason to share the rewards with those who were less lucky.

The most important rule

While these rules are important, the number one rule of success remains to do what has intrinsic value to us. Since there is no guarantee of success in any endeavor, only a high chance of failure, doing something only to become rich, respected, or gain something else is futile – it is extrinsic. Regardless of what we do, we will most likely gain nothing aside from the work we put in. If this work has intrinsic value to us, and if we can use the experience in our next endeavors, we achieve two advantages:

1. We can gradually build success

When we use doing what has intrinsic value to us as a compass to guide us through our lives, every new experience – professional as well as private – will add to the experiences we made before. It will be in a similar field regarding similar values. Over time, these related experiences will accumulate to a wealth of knowledge surrounding the topics and values we care about, helping us to make better decisions and achieve greater levels of success. Without passion as our compass, our experiences will be in fields too different to combine. When we sell insurance in our day job and are passionate about space flight when we come home, there are few synergy effects. As passion has no influence on our professional career, we put in too little time and effort to achieve high levels of mastery, and success keeps eluding us.

2. We are happy

It is impossible to force success. While we stumble from one unpredictable, chaotic experience to the next, we might as well be happy. Doing what has intrinsic value to us will help us do exactly that, making us more successful than any amount of money ever could.

Perfectionism is hell

This approach to trying new things requires us to let go of our perfectionism. When we try something new, we are insecure about how things will turn out. Even though we try to convince ourselves and others that we have found the right idea for this time and place, we know that we can only guess, at best. To deal with the insecurity, the fear of failure, and the potential shame we could feel, many of us invest too much money in an unproven idea, succumb to perfectionism, or fall for a similar false replacement.

While these false replacements, disguised as efforts to be more successful or generate a better product, are socially accepted, they are an attempt to deal with our insecurities. We think that we can force success by pouring large amounts of time, money, and effort into an endeavor. In reality, though, these attempts rarely generate any positive results. Of course, we have to reach a certain standard of quality to be successful at anything, but investing a lot of money to get a professional logo design fails to help our blogs to be ranked high on Google. Similarly, perfectionism and over-investing often miss the areas most critical to our success, focusing instead on minor issues that barely impact the outcome but give us the opportunity to waste endless hours of work and streams of money.

Recognizing and eliminating those false replacements early will save us a lot of time and money, increasing our happiness, and, strangely enough, our chances of eventual success. Since there is no way of knowing whether an idea's time has come, we have to try many ideas quickly. Perfectionism and over-investing will only delay this process. If failure is inevitable due to bad circumstances, failing as quickly as possible will help us try the next idea sooner and find success earlier. This applies to all aspects of our lives:

- Regardless of how much we try to find the perfect relationship, long-lasting happiness always requires a great deal of luck. There's nothing we can do to avoid sickness, to anticipate all events that could make us and our partners grow apart, or to make sure that our partners have no dark secrets hidden from us. If we try to prevent these events, we destroy the relationship or waste our time doubting everything.

- Whether we die in transport or not is largely due to chance and events we can neither predict nor influence. Avoiding airplanes, the subway, or ships are false replacements for a lack of certainty.

- Regardless of how perfectly we plan a wedding, Christmas, or any other event – whether these events go well or not is largely due to chance. Whether our guests show up in a good or bad mood is beyond our influence, as is whether they get along and whether someone drinks too much. Trying to prevent these events will kill the mood more than if these events occur.

- We can't guarantee that our children will grow up to be who we want them to be. Trying to force them into a certain direction will hurt them more than letting them find their own way.

Self-Help Deception #37: Great effort can force success.

Conclusion

1. The major factor to great success is luck – we have to be in a good situation, meet the right people and have a million other things go right for us.
2. There are many ways to stop ourselves from being successful, but not a single way to force success. We have to accept the fact that we will most likely fail in most of our endeavors and must plan accordingly.
3. When we do what has intrinsic value to us, we are already successful – we accumulate knowledge, and we are happy. Over time, we gradually become better and as successful as our situation allows.

Further reading

Malcolm Gladwell: Outliers.

A detailed analysis of the outstanding circumstances that created great successes, the effort it took to take advantage of these circumstances, but also of how many people failed in spite of similar or even bigger effort. Reading this book can help us get a more realistic outlook on life and find a better place for ourselves in this world.

Chapter 17

How can we stop self-sabotage?

"In order to understand, I destroyed myself."
FERNANDO PESSOA

When I first entered politics, I was young and idealistic. I wanted to help people create a better world. Over time, I witnessed many situations where other members of my party did what helped themselves but harmed the party and thus destroyed everything we had worked for. As I began to realize that we were unable to help anybody because we always got in our own way, my frustration grew, and I started to neglect my duties. Instead of quitting politics immediately, I gradually reduced the quality of my work until it became apparent that my chances for re-election had faded – I sabotaged my way out of politics.

From time to time, we all sabotage ourselves. There is something we need to do and that we could easily do, but we just are incapable of acting on it, or we do a bad job at a task we could knock out of the park easily. So far, we have found plenty of reasons that explain a large part of these instances. Sometimes we act dumb to gain the approval of others; sometimes we avoid a task because we are afraid to fail. There are, however, plenty of cases these answers fail to explain. When our bosses ask us to do an easy task, we are neither afraid (we know we can do it) nor will underperforming help us to be accepted (our boss might get angry at us), but sometimes we sabotage ourselves anyway. We would rather waste time doing nothing than perform an essential, easy task. Why? What is our ego trying to achieve?

Self-help literature calls this phenomenon self-sabotage, presenting plenty of strategies to overcome it but no explanation of where it comes from. It is time to shed light on the topic and find out what self-sabotage is, what we can learn from it, and whether this behavior deserves to be called "sabotage." Let's answer these questions.

Why do we sabotage ourselves?

Self-sabotage is our ego's attempt to eliminate our false replacements. To use a simple example from an earlier chapter, people who have given up on finding true love often get a cat to replace the feeling of love they are missing. This false replacement can trick our essential needs, but it can't trick our non-essential needs, contribution, and growth. Our non-essential needs work on too long of a timescale to allow us to create a false replacement. When we get a cat instead of starting a family, we can feel love, but contribution and growth feel different. Buying our cat a new litter box creates a less rewarding sense of contribution than teaching our kids how to ride a bike and how to live a good life.

Eventually, our ego realizes this problem. That is where self-sabotage starts. The super-ego begins to understand that what we do is incapable of meeting its needs. Consequently, the super-ego sounds the alarm – it encourages us to start finding our true selves. Most people might be unable to articulate this thought clearly, but they somehow feel that what they are doing reflects a false self and that they want to get away from it. Nonetheless, our id is perfectly fine with what we are doing – our false replacements can satisfy its needs. In the long run, fulfilling the super-ego's plan would make the id happy, too, but the id is indifferent to the long run. The id wants to meet its needs here and now. Starting a long, hard journey to find our true selves sounds too risky for the id.

In this situation, the ego faces a dilemma. It knows the super-ego is right, and that it should give up the false replacement, but it also needs the false replacement to satisfy our essential needs. To solve this problem, the ego must find a way to eliminate what it can't give up. Without a constructive option, the ego wants the false replacement to be taken from us. To create this situation, the ego starts to sabotage us. Self-sabotage is an attempt to eliminate false replacements we can't give up.

Self-Help Deception #38: Self-sabotage is a sign of weakness.

Should we stop self-sabotage?

When we understand self-sabotage as the ego's attempt to eliminate false replacements, we realize why most conventional ways of dealing with self-sabotage are fundamentally flawed. They are an attempt to brainwash ourselves into holding on to our false replacements. These attempts are unable to create positive results. Our false replacements will never satisfy all our needs, which is why we will always keep sabotaging ourselves if we continue living our false replacements. We can create much better, happier lives by letting the false replacements go, getting back to our true selves. The only way to live a life without self-sabotage is to live our true selves – to identify the false replacement, to find the part of our true selves we suppressed to create it, and to find a way to live this part again.

Self-Help Deception #39: We should deal with self-sabotage by finding ways to do what we have no motivation to do.

When we sabotage our success at work, for example, we use our job as a false replacement in some way. Of course, there are millions of possibilities, but it could be that we took the wrong job to begin with:

- Maybe we wanted to impress our parents, friends, or a love interest.
- Maybe we wanted the safest job possible.
- Maybe we thought we lacked what it took to pursue our true passion.

Whatever it was, we are now stuck in a job that fails to satisfy our needs for growth and contribution – we do not grow as a person, and we do not contribute to what's important to us. We can't solve this fundamental problem by trying to be better at a job we hate. We can only solve this fundamental problem by finding a way to satisfy our needs, a solution that enables us to use our skills to contribute to our passions.

Imagine a writer who is passionate about space exploration. When she started writing about NASA's newest missions for her school's paper, she loved what she did, so much, that she went on to study journalism. After college, this writer's parents told her about a job vacancy at the local small-town newspaper. She wanted to make them proud, so she took it. For the last ten years, she has been writing about neighborhood feuds, car accidents, and missing dogs. Now she starts to hate her job and sabotage herself. She finishes her stories after the deadline, she complains about her job to her boss; she has become unfriendly and grumpy. What should she do? Should this writer employ self-help strategies to keep a job she hates? Would that not only mask her problem? Her real issue is not that she is bad at her job, it is that she hates her job. Forcing herself to be more effective at something she has no motivation to do is destructive, requiring her to suppress a part of who she is, creating new false replacements.

There are plenty of constructive alternatives to resolve this conflict:

- Most obviously, the writer could quit her job and write for a magazine on space flight. That might not be easy, though, as jobs in specialized papers could be rare and low paying.
- She could also keep her job and, as a hobby, use her writing talents to start a blog on space flight, contribute to her local observatory's newsletter, or write for a non-profit organization that wants to educate the public about space flight. Now, her first job would have become a way to pay the bills while she uses her skills and reputation to work on her true passion.
- She could ask her editor if he would allow her to write a monthly column on space flight. If he does, she can use her job to contribute to her passion. She might still get some assignments that she finds impossible to enjoy, but, at least, she now has one thing to be proud of.

The first option would be ideal, but even the second and third options would create a shift in meaning that brings her job in line with what has intrinsic value to her. She needs to be good at her job because it enables her to live her passion. That shift will help control her self-sabotage problems.

Now, her ego no longer has to find a way to eliminate her job, because it is no longer a false replacement – she has integrated it into her true self.

This example shows how we can solve the problem of self-sabotage constructively. When we recognize a false replacement in our lives, we need to eliminate it, or our minds will try to eliminate it through self-sabotage, which is the worst way possible. Most of the time, however, we can avoid changing our entire lives. When we have done a false replacement for quite a while, we automatically have acquired some skills. Destroying anything that is connected to our false replacement would throw these skills away. Often, that is unnecessary. When we incorporate the false replacement into our true selves, we can use the skills we have gained to our benefit.

Over time, our writer's new hobby or column might lead to more opportunities in space flight writing. Maybe she meets other spaceflight enthusiasts, maybe someone needs a writer with experience in space flight writing and she can start pursuing her passion full-time. On the other hand, she might remain a happy space-flight writer in her spare time – which would not be the worst result either.

The important thing to realize is that the problem rarely lies with what we do, but with why we do it. Writing, for example, can be good or bad, depending on what we write about. When we use writing about a topic we are not passionate about to enable us to write about a topic we are passionate about, we have realigned what used to be a false replacement with our true selves. It is important to find a solution, a way out. Often, we can avoid what makes us unhappy with small changes, giving ourselves a new perspective we can gradually build a new life on.

Conclusion

1. Self-sabotage is an attempt to eliminate false replacements.
2. We can cure self-sabotage by freeing ourselves from our false replacements, by living our true selves, not by using techniques that keep these false replacements alive.
3. Eliminating false replacements doesn't require us to change our entire lives. Often, we can restructure our lives and integrate what we already have into our true selves, starting a slow but rewarding growth process.

Chapter 18

Do our thoughts influence reality?

When I was in fourth grade, I was in love with a girl. The problem was that when boys and girls had to line up according to height before the start of PE class, we stood next to each other – because she was the tallest girl and I was the shortest boy. While we liked each other, she never wanted to go out with a boy who was a good few inches shorter than her. Every day, I wished I were taller as desperately as only a young boy in love could wish for anything. And, since my hopes to magically grow two inches were limited, I also wished that she would go out with me regardless of our height difference. Of course, neither happened. But why? According to self-help books such as Rhonda Byrne's *The Secret*, we simply need to believe in our success, and it will happen. Other books such as Bruce Lipton's *The Biology of Belief* suggest that our thoughts can influence our DNA. If our thoughts have such big power to shape our lives then why did my desperate wish to grow not change my DNA? Why did my belief that this girl and I were perfect for each other fail to change her mind about me? Was my belief too weak or is the entire concept a lie?

Is there disconfirming evidence?

To prove that our thoughts influence reality, books proclaiming this idea deliver many examples of success they attribute to positivity. Rock stars, athletes, business people, inventors, politicians, etc. – many of the greatest people of their fields had positive attitudes. Unquestionably, a positive attitude and a positive expectancy of life are a common trait of many successful people. Nonetheless, this fails to prove that positivity is in any way connected to success. The problem with most of these books' nature is their authors' highly unscientific approach. They first came up with a theory and then searched for examples to prove this theory. If they can find enough examples, and pseudo-evidence can be found for even the weirdest theories, they weave them into a well-sounding web, wrap a fancy name around it, and publish it as a book, seemingly proving exactly what they wanted to prove all along.

In reality, though, these books prove nothing. We can only evaluate a theory scientifically if we try to disprove it. Instead of trying to find evidence that seems to confirm our belief, we must try to find evidence that disconfirms it. When we find disconfirming evidence, we need to abandon our theory or, at least, refine it to explain all cases. Only if we are unable to find any disconfirming evidence, can we accept our theory.

This fundamentally necessary step never happens in books such as *The Secret* or *The Biology of Belief* – for good reason. Essentially, both books claim that positive thoughts automatically create what we believe, either through changes in our DNA or quantum mechanics. To find disconfirming evidence for this theory, we must look for two types of cases:

- People who succeeded despite a negative attitude.
- People who failed despite a positive attitude.

Let's start with the first point, people who succeeded despite a negative attitude. Think of your high-school football team. Which players became team captains? Who made it to college and/or the pros? Those with the most positive attitudes? Rarely. In almost every case, there were many players on the team who had at least as positive an attitude as those who succeeded at higher levels of play. But not all of them made it. The many examples of professional athletes who get into legal troubles, have mental health issues, or simply prefer partying to practicing is undeniable evidence that a positive attitude is not what distinguishes professional athletes from the rest of us. Pelé, Joe Montana, Babe Ruth, Wayne Gretzky – there is no sign that it was an especially positive attitude that separated these great athletes from other less successful players.

Outside of athletics, we can find many more examples. After Albert Einstein, one of the greatest geniuses in human history, died in 1955, his brain was stolen and analyzed. Scientific studies suggest that in Einstein's brain regions involved in speech and language were smaller than in an average brain while regions involved with numerical and spatial processing were larger. Other studies suggest an increased number of glial cells and a stronger connection between both hemispheres of the brain. Apparently, Einstein's brain offered unique conditions for highly abstract thinking – conditions that were more important for Einstein's success than his attitude, which was no more positive than the attitude of most other scientists.

In business, too, a positive attitude shows no correlation to success. Studies have shown that CEOs are depressed at twice the rate of the general public. According to British Journalist Jon Ronson (*The Psychopath Test: A Journey Through the Madness Industry*), 4 percent of all CEOs qualify as psychopaths – 4 times the average of the population at large. There's plenty of scientific evidence to suggest that successful businessmen are no more positive than the average person, more likely they are even less positive.

Neither Bill Gates nor Steve Jobs nor any other great businessman, athlete, or otherwise successful person appears to be exceptionally positive. Successful people have all kinds of character traits, much like any other group of people. Some of these traits are positive; some are negative. Focusing on a single good trait might explain a few success stories, but it can never explain the entire bandwidth of human performance.

It's impossible to explain success with positive thoughts – there's no correlation. Of course, being overly pessimistic is similarly destructive. Once again, the most important key to a good life is a realistic evaluation of our situation, our abilities, and our chances to achieve something. Anything that distracts us from this realistic evaluation, either in a positive or negative way, decreases our chances to be successful. Additionally, there is not a single shred of evidence that our thoughts influence the world. All the pseudo-evidence given in books proclaiming this idea is either taken out of context or a downright lie. Our thoughts only exist in our minds; they have no direct influence on the world. We can only influence the world through our actions.

Is skill more important than positivity?

If positivity fails to explain success, then what does? Aside from a good portion of luck and the right circumstances, the most significant difference between people who succeed at something and those who do not succeed is skill, not attitude. We all intuitively know that. Who would you rather have flying your plane? A clueless guy with a positive attitude or a skilled pilot who hates his job? Any sane person would choose the latter. Who would you rather have performing your surgery? A positive butcher or a suicidal doctor? The law of attraction is complete nonsense.

Every day, we are reminded that a positive attitude is far from enough to accomplish anything. There are plenty of athletes with negative attitudes, but there's no athlete without skill. There are plenty of depressed successful people, but not one successful person who has no idea what they are doing. There's great art from people who killed themselves, but no great art from people without talent.

A philosophy of life that ignores skill is nonsense. It can only lead us down a dead end. Sooner or later, our lack of skills will keep us from advancing further, from doing what we want. Then, we have invested a lot of time, effort, and, in many cases, money into something we never had a chance to accomplish.

Why do people believe in positivity?

The belief that a positive attitude can magically generate success is tempting but ridiculous. When we believe that we can accomplish anything by being positive, we feel certainty, possibility, and significance. Now we only need to tie the possibility of achieving anything to a fantasy that makes us feel loved, and we have satisfied all four of our basic needs.

When something has the power to satisfy all our needs, we will believe it – unless we have something that is more important for our needs. Unfortunately, most people do not value science, logic, and reason as their highest ideals, which explains why many of them believe in positivity as the determining factor to success despite plenty of evidence to the contrary – it helps them feel better.

So is attitude worthless?

In life, those who succeed are those who use their skills best, not those with the most positive attitudes. But does that mean attitude is worthless? Well, not quite. Every year, hundreds of young hopefuls who are about to enter the NFL draft are invited to the NFL scouting combine, where their physical abilities are put to the test. Every year, the combine results cause NFL scouts to classify some players as a perfect athletic fit for the NFL. On draft day, these players are usually first off the board. Strangely enough, though, their immense physical ability is often insufficient to translate into success on the field.

In the 1998 NFL draft, the first overall pick was decided between Peyton Manning and Ryan Leaf, both quarterbacks. Ryan Leaf had the better physical attributes – he was stronger, had a stronger arm, and better throwing mechanics than Manning. But it was Manning who had a Hall of Fame career while Leaf never achieved any success. Every year, athletes of all sports create results that can't be explained by talent alone. Even in fields where natural ability is highly important, we find that natural ability alone is insufficient to explain which players will be successful and which will not.

Outside of sports, we find the same results. Albert Einstein's brain was ideal for advanced mathematical thinking. But was it unique? Probably not. In a world of seven billion people, we have to assume that there are many people with equal or even better genetic preconditions for mathematical genius. Einstein, however, developed his genius better than anybody else. Charles Darwin had a younger cousin, Sir Francis Galton. By all accounts, Galton was the superior scientific intellect. At a very young age, people started to praise Galton as a genius to come, and he did have a successful career, but it was Darwin, a man who described himself as unable to follow a longer train of thought, who became one of the scientists that changed our entire worldview. Why?

As it seems, skill alone fails to explain success sufficiently. Not everybody who has talent succeeds. Apparently, some people develop their talent and some do not. Often, people with less talent reach a higher level of skill than those with a higher level of talent. To create a valuable philosophy of life, we need to explain this connection and find the factor that turns talent into skill. Then we can use this factor to our advantage.

Many of the factors that stop talented people from developing their skills are environmental circumstances nobody can influence. When we are born in a country without a working school system, even the biggest genius is lost. Similarly, disease and war can wipe out our skills before we can develop them.

Inequality, a restrictive environment, and limiting ideologies and religions can also stop us from developing our skills. The smartest woman in the world, for example, can accomplish nothing if she is denied an education.

Nonetheless, we have to assess that highly skilled people often had success despite the worst kind of circumstances. Michael Faraday, for example, was an English scientist who revolutionized our understanding of electromagnetism and electrochemistry with such great discoveries as electromagnetic induction, diamagnetism, and electrolysis. Faraday came from a simple background. He was the son of a blacksmith's apprentice and received little formal education. Faraday was far from being in the ideal position to become one of the most influential scientists in history, but he beat the odds while equally skilled people with ideal circumstances failed. At the time, British universities were filled with bright young students contemplating the same issues as Faraday. None of them came up with nearly as paradigm-shifting results as he did.

History offers plenty of similar examples:

- Thomas Edison was one of the most prolific inventors in history, holding 1,093 patents and creating such world-changing inventions as electric power, electric light, and the phonograph. He only received three months of schooling and was later home schooled by his mother, mainly relying on only two books.
- Albert Einstein was working as a third grade technical expert at the patent office to support his wife and two sons when he published four world-changing papers in 1905, among them the theory of special relativity.
- Warren Buffett, the world's most successful financial investor, was born and raised in Omaha, Nebraska far away from Wall Street and the financial epicenters of the world.
- The Wright brothers were working on printing presses, bicycles, and motors in their shop and had no large financial backing like many of the competitors in the race for the first powered flight.

We can find similar patterns in the lives of most success stories. None of these future successes were born into desperate circumstances where success was impossible. At the same time, none of them were born with a silver spoon in their mouth. Therefore, outer circumstances and skill are an insufficient explanation for their success. There has to be another factor. What? Is it time to bring back positivity? Well, not so fast.

Passion as the second secret to success

Positivity is a strange concept. It implies that we can be positive for all our lives. We all know this is impossible. Negative thoughts are a normal element of life. While dwelling in them helps nobody, neither does ignoring them. Negative emotions help us discover wrong beliefs and eliminate them – a vital step to success and happiness.

Nonetheless, talent alone will get us nowhere. We need to develop our talents into unique skills. That requires determination. Positivity is a failed attempt to explain the force that helps us make this transformation. We need a better concept than positivity. We need something that keeps us going in the same way positivity is supposed to, but allows for realistic self-evaluation. Something that pushes us through adversity. Something that develops our skills even under difficult circumstances. This concept is passion:

- Ryan Leaf never had a passion for playing in the NFL. He snapped at reporters, felt haunted, and wanted to be left alone. Peyton Manning does have a passion for playing in the NFL. So do Tom Brady and Drew Brees, and so did Brett Favre and Joe Montana.
- Albert Einstein was passionate about physics, and so are Neil deGrasse Tyson and Bill Nye.
- Steve Jobs was passionate about designing revolutionary consumer electronics, Warren Buffett about investing, and Bruce Springsteen about helping people with his music.

Passion and skill are the two elements of success. Without skill, any attempt at success is futile, but passion adds intrinsic value to what we do, enabling us to turn mere talents into fully developed skills. Concepts such as the law of attraction mistake the positive attitude passion creates as the cause of success, ignoring that positivity shows no correlation with success. Even combining our strengths and passions fails to guarantee that we will change the world. It even fails to guarantee that we will be recognized as successful in the eyes of others. But it does guarantee that we will have the most success possible and that we will be as happy as we can be. That is all we can ask of a realistic philosophy of life.

Conclusion

1. Positivity doesn't help us to be successful. It is incapable of changing our DNA or influencing reality in any way.
2. The secret to success is combining our strengths and passions. While passion is often mistaken as positivity, it is fundamentally different.
3. A realistic outlook on life helps us make good decisions on how to combine our strengths and passions. Neither an overly positive attitude nor an overly negative attitude will help us be happier or more successful.

Chapter 19

How to make better decisions

Most negative events in my life have been the result of my own bad decisions. I knew exactly what I wanted and what was right, but I was unable to act accordingly. Often, faulty logic was the cause of these bad decisions. In earlier chapters, we already touched on examples of faulty logic such as the survivorship bias and the self-serving bias and their negative effects on our quality of life. While living our true selves can help us avoid most cases of faulty logic from the start, many cases of faulty logic are hard to discover and can easily sneak into our lives without us noticing. To avoid this problem, this chapter will introduce more examples of faulty logic and show you how to avoid them. For more examples of faulty logic, I recommend Rolf Dobelli's books *The Art of Thinking Clearly* and *The Art of Acting Clearly* which each list 50 examples of faulty logic, and are where most of the examples in this chapter are taken from.

The sunk cost fallacy

Not so long ago, I owned a 20-year old Chrysler Town & Country van. Its condition was questionable, to say the least. Every time I turned the key, I was afraid it wouldn't start, and I had to invest multiple thousands of Euros every year to keep it running. Even though it would have been much cheaper to get a better car, the more I invested into Bruce, as I called the Chrysler, the more I fell in love with it. Every time I drove somewhere without breaking down, I gave the car a pat on the hood, thanking it for its trusty service. In hindsight, that was ridiculous. I fell for the sunk cost fallacy.

When we invest a lot into something but the returns fail to justify our high investment, we feel ashamed for our stupidity and create a false replacement. Our mind tries to explain our high investment by attributing special properties to what we invested in. Most of the time, this property is love:

- I convinced myself that I loved my car and that my annual investment was well worth the money, despite all evidence pointing to the contrary. Similarly, when we sell our cars, we often overestimate their value because we know how much we invested in them.
- When we are in love but someone takes advantage of us without giving anything back, we sometimes try to justify our investment by convincing ourselves that our partner is "the one" and that we need them to be happy, which is complete nonsense.

- Groups often use a form of pledging to increase the members' investment in the group. Attempting to validate their high investment by attributing special attributes to the group, pledging creates committed, devoted members.
- Obstacle runs such as Tough Mudder hand out small rewards to their contestants. These rewards, headbands and the like, are worthless, but they give the contestants a chance to project their investment into them. Without these rewards, the contestants might question how much sense there is in paying a lot of money to wade through mud and get electro shocks.

The sunk cost fallacy is a special form of cognitive dissonance, a false replacement we talked about in Chapter 5 (*"Why we do what makes us unhappy"*).

The introspection illusion

Swedish psychologist Petter Johansson showed his test subjects two portraits. The contestants had to pick the photo they found more attractive. Johannson then gave the picture to his subjects and asked them to explain why they chose this picture. Unbeknown to the subjects, Johannson exchanged the two pictures and showed the subjects the picture they selected to be less attractive. Failing to recognize the deception, most test subjects argued their case, coming up with all kinds of reasons why the portrait in front of them is the more attractive one. Apparently, their mindset had changed. They were no longer trying to make a decision, only to justify the decision they had already made. They were trying to satisfy their needs by proving that they made a good decision, which became more important than actually making a good decision.

The same illusion happens to each of us in our daily lives. When we question the motives of our behavior, we often overestimate their purity. If someone questions our false replacements, we react destructively in one of three ways:

- We think the other person lacks information. We try to educate them, even if they are indifferent to what we have to say.
- When we find that the other person has all the information but still disagrees with us, we assume the person is an idiot. This explains a good part of government initiatives to protect the "stupid" consumers from themselves.
- When we find that the other person has all the information and is intelligent, we assume that they are evil. This can lead to some problems:
  1. Political conflicts often get overly aggressive because both sides clearly have some intelligent people that possess all the necessary

information. Since we overestimate the purity of our own motives, we assume that the other side must be evil.

2. Soccer fans fight each other because they fail to understand how they use their own overzealous fan culture as a false replacement for a lack of significance and love/connection. When they meet fans of another team, these fans question their false replacement. Since other fans clearly have all the information and can't all be stupid, each fan concludes that the other side is evil and must be fought.

Even if we do not recognize our own false replacements, we can detect them with these emotions. Whenever we get angry at something that didn't attack us or when we try to diminish someone by ridiculing them, we act on a false replacement. Our true selves promote what they believe in but allow others their own beliefs. They understand that we are genetically different and can't all believe the same things. Our true selves only use violence as a last option in defense, never in attack.

The new book bias

As I write these lines, I have 11 books on my desk, all of them half-read. Whenever I see a new book that promises great insights, I buy it and put the book I'm currently reading on hold. I fear that I could miss a good idea, that I could live the rest of my life not knowing what I desperately need to know and so easily could have learned. Since I have a rough idea of what my current book is about but no idea what this new book could reveal to me, I keep jumping from one book to the next. Of course, this behavior is a false replacement. I'm trying to fill a lack of certainty and possibility by reading 11 books at the same time, an endeavor that will inevitably fail and leave me more uncertain than before.

Many of us make similar mistakes in our daily lives:

- We date multiple people at the same time, only to be overwhelmed by the situation.
- We try to keep all our career choices open, only to find that trying to do three things simultaneously means that we can do nothing right.
- We keep friendships alive that have clearly run their course, only to find that they take time away from the friendships we enjoy.

To lead good, happy lives, we need to be able to focus on the book most important to us now. This means to stop reading some and never to start reading others. When we dwell only in possibility, we get nowhere. Doing what has intrinsic value to us helps us decide which books are right for us. It gives us a clear selection compass for which direction we should go in and which we should avoid.

The accurate memory illusion

In 1973, American political scientist Gregory Markus asked 3,000 test subjects to give their opinion on controversial political topics. Ten years later, he surveyed the same people on the same topics. They had to list their opinion ten years ago and their current opinion. The results showed that people claimed that their opinion ten years ago matched their current opinion – which was far from true. Their real opinion ten years ago had little in common with what they now claimed it to have been. Apparently, their minds reinterpreted the past in a way that helped them believe that they were always right.

The day after the Space Shuttle Challenger disintegrated during launch; American psychologist Ulrich Neisser asked his students to write down what they did, where they were, and what they thought when the tragedy happened. Three years later, he asked them the same questions. Only 7 percent of the students gave the same answers, 50 percent of the answers differed in two-thirds of all points, and 25 percent differed in every single point – the number of students with a completely inaccurate recollection was four times as high as the number of students with an accurate recollection. Apparently, even trusting so-called *flashbulb memories* of highly important events in our lives creates a false sense of mental accuracy. Our recollections of our greatest triumphs and greatest defeats, our biggest surprises and our biggest shocks are most likely all inaccurate.

Our memories are highly unreliable. They tend to reinterpret past events with what we learned now, distorting them more and more. Of all the things we think we remember, the majority happened quite differently. In a complex world that we hardly understand, reinterpreting the past helps us feel certainty, possibility, and significance, which is more important to our minds than the truth. In the present, this causes us to overestimate our ability to deal with events and gets us into situations beyond our capabilities.

This way of thinking is a false replacement, a special form of the self-serving bias. To stop it, we can keep a journal. When we experience important events, we can write down how we feel and why we feel this way. Years later, we can go back to these notes and understand our thought process better, which helps us make better decisions. We also get a feeling for how badly we are at evaluating events, and learn not to overestimate our current opinions.

Ambiguity intolerance

In 1961, Harvard psychology professor Daniel Ellsberg described this experiment: A box (box A) contains 100 balls. 50 of them are red, 50 are black. A second box (box B) also contains 100 balls, but you do not know how many of them are red and how many black. You are now given the choice to draw a ball from box A or box B. If you draw a red ball you get $100. Which box would you choose? If you are like most people, you choose box A. Now you get offered the same $100 if you draw a black ball. Which box do you choose now? If you are like most people, you once again choose box A.

This makes no sense. Box B has either more black balls or more red balls than box A. When we pick from box A in both cases; we reduce our chances. If we picked from box A with our first try, we should pick from box B on the second try. Most of us decide to pick from box A twice because we know the odds. There are fifty black balls and fifty red balls – we *know* that we have a 50/50 chance. We prefer known odds over unknown odds, even if the unknown odds might be significantly better.

Our intolerance of ambiguity can make our lives worse. In our modern world, we often deal with situations too complex to generate exact odds. We can estimate our risk to suffer from cancer in our lifetime, our chances to win the lottery, and our chances to die in a plane crash – there are millions of similar instances, which allow us to make a good prediction. However, we are unable to predict whether the stock market will go up or down over the next year, whether our currency will rise or fall, or whether the economy will improve or get worse. There are too many factors involved, and there has never been a situation similar to the one we experience now, which makes a prediction impossible.

Most of the events in our lives do not allow for exact odds. They are uncertain, and there is a good chance anything could happen. This uncertainty is a normal part of life, but it hurts our need for certainty ("I know what will happen"), possibility ("I can deal with the current situation"), and significance ("I know what's going on"). To cope with these hurt feelings, we invent false replacements. We start to believe in conspiracy theories, to oversimplify the world, or to withdraw from uncertain situations.

All of these false replacements make our lives worse. We can create better, happier lives by learning to accept ambiguity and dealing with it in a realistic way, by doing what has intrinsic value to us and not worrying about the outcomes we can neither control nor predict.

Neomania

Did you see Back to the Future II where Marty and Doc travel to the year 2015? In the film's version of the future, cars can fly, there are hoverboards, power-lacing shoes, auto-adjusting and auto-drying jackets, video glasses, and so on. How many of these things came true? None. Similarly, people in the 1950s expected the future to bring plastic houses, space vacations, and nuclear reactors for every house. These visions didn't come true either. We still have metal cars, stone houses, and dream of vacations in Hawaii.

It seems that we consistently overvalue the importance of what is new. In the 50s, plastic, rockets, and nuclear power were big news, so people thought that these inventions would dominate the future. The writers of Back to the Future II also overvalued what was new at their time – modern fabrics, electronics, and computer games.

Our tendency to overvalue what is new is a false replacement. Being faced with an infinitely complex future that is impossible to predict hurts our essential needs. We feel uncertain, unconnected, and insignificant. Since we are unable to accept that we have no idea how the future will turn out, we create the best version we can by extending our current developmental trajectory into the future. This can lead to bad decisions.

- We might invest a lot of money in stocks of a company with a hot new product, only to find that this company will suffer the same fate as so many hot new companies before.
- Early adopters who always buy the newest electronic gadget gladly pay two or three times more for something with little added value than for an almost identical product, only because the more expensive product is new. They justify the additional cost with the world-changing consequences they expect their newest device will have.

We can avoid neomania by evaluating new technologies realistically. A technology that has been around for hundreds of years will very likely be around for another hundred years. Something that is new today will most likely fade away as quickly as it appeared. For the few times it will not, we can still get the new product two years later when it is significantly cheaper.

The constant improvement bias

Imagine two friends playing two rounds of bowling. In the first round, one friend beats the other by 50 pins. Now the winner finds out that the guy playing in the lane next to him is the current world champion. He quickly asks for a few tips. Which of the friends will win the second round? The guy who already lost the first round by 50 pins or the guy who won in a landslide and got tips from the world champion? The funny thing is, in many cases the guy who lost the first round is going to win the second round. Why is that?

Let's say the world champion has 100 percent of the skill anyone can have in bowling. The two friends play just for fun, so they have 40 and 30 percent of the skill. The friend with 40 percent of the skill wins round one. Now he gets some tips from the world champion. Eventually, these tips will allow him to perfect his technique and get to 60 or 70 percent of the skill in bowling. For now, however, he has very little experience with the new techniques, preventing them from aiding his skill right away. He has to train them first. The old techniques he's giving up, however, subtract from his skill.

These techniques may be worse than what he just learned, but at least, he trained them for years. In the short run, his skill will drop from 40 percent to 20 percent. All of a sudden he's a weaker player than the friend he humiliated in round one and probably will lose round two.

In our lives, we experience many situations where we know that we have to change something to grow and get better. When we trade what we are experienced at for what's new to us, we are bound to get worse in the beginning. Now we have two options:

1. We can think that our changes are worthless, and go back to what we did before. This may seem easier but will forever keep us from getting better and achieving higher goals.
2. We can push through. Then, we will eventually become good at what we have learned. We may suffer in the beginning, but in the end, we can reap the rewards.

In the long run, the second option will make our lives better – but we are also more reluctant to go down this road. Many of us use our skills as a false replacement. For example, the better bowler of our two friends could use his bowling victories as a false replacement for:

- Certainty: when we bowl, I will win.
- Possibility: my skills might make my friends or beautiful women admire me.
- Significance: I'm the best.
- Love/connection: my friends would like to be as good as I am.

Asking us to become worse at any skill or ability for a while means asking us to abandon a proven method to satisfy our essential needs. As we saw in Chapter 12 ("How to evaluate ourselves reasonably"), distant, abstract needs are less attractive to our minds than nearer, concrete needs. Therefore, the concrete method to satisfy our needs will always seem more attractive than the abstract, long-term goal of getting better. We can overcome this problem by erasing the need for the short-term false replacement, allowing us to pursue the highly rewarding long-term goal without any risk to our essential needs.

This process is not limited to bowling:

- To find an intrinsically rewarding job, we might need to quit our current job and risk failure in our new job. When we hang on to the perceived safety of our current environment, we can never find the work we love.
- To find an intrinsically rewarding relationship, we might need to end our current relationship and be single for a while. When we cling to the small rewards of our current relationship, we can never find true satisfaction.

We can only allow better things into our lives if we are willing to let old, worse things go – and with them the false replacements they were tied to. Most people want to get better constantly. Every time they regress they abandon what they were doing, even if they were on the right path. Avoiding this mistake can help us lead better, happier lives.

One word of caution, though: while the constant improvement bias applies to our lives, we should beware of politicians and CEOs who use a similar rhetoric. Often, they try to buy time and mask the fact that they have no idea what they are doing. Anybody running a government or business should have at least some ideas to improve the situation quickly.

Domain dependence

In almost every country, doctors rank among the professionals with the highest percentage of smokers. Nobody understands better than doctors that smoking is a slow killer without positive effects, but this knowledge fails to lead to better decisions. Psychologists call this effect *domain dependence*. Our knowledge is so intensely linked to one domain that we are incapable of transporting it to another, even if both domains are obviously connected. Often, this effect even stops us from translating our theoretical knowledge into actions.

The influence of domain dependence reaches beyond doctors:

- Most critics are precise and knowledgeable in their analysis but almost incapable of doing what they critique. Art critics are unable to draw or create a good painting, film critics can't make a good movie, and music critics can't write a good song.
- In 1990, Harry Markowitz received the Nobel Prize in economics for his theory of portfolio selection. Markowitz later admitted that he neglected to use his own genius model in favor of simply splitting his private investments 50/50 between stocks and bonds.
- As statistics show all over the world, police officers commit more crimes than the average person.

These examples show that knowledge alone doesn't lead to better decisions. Often, we know the right thing to do, but we fail to act on this knowledge. Why?

Our actions are determined by our four basic needs: certainty, possibility, love/connection, and significance. If necessary, these needs can overrule our knowledge. Imagine a doctor. He and his wife were already smokers long before they met. Lately, they have both been so busy that their mutual smoke breaks are the only time when they can talk. For this doctor, stopping smoking is not a question of knowledge. The doctor knows that smoking will kill him, but he might fear that to stop smoking could estrange him from his wife and ultimately destroy their marriage.

The thought of a destroyed marriage has great power over the doctor. If his wife left him, his need for love/connection would go unsatisfied, and he would lose the significance of being a husband. That hurts his needs for certainty and possibility. Losing his wife would create a void in all of the doctor's needs. As unlikely as the thought might be, its consequences are so excruciating that he has to be sure to prevent it. Subconsciously, his feelings will overrule his knowledge, and he will keep smoking.

Of course, there are other decisions available. Our doctor could convince his wife to stop smoking together. They would need to form a replacement habit which would give them something else to do. They could enjoy a glass of wine together every day, for example. Our doctor's marriage would be safe, and he would be saving his life and also his wife's – clearly the better decision.

The oversimplification trap

We are often overwhelmed by the seemingly endless possibilities of a decision. This leads to oversimplifications. We only focus on the most obvious criteria. When choosing a partner, the thousands of possible partners that social media and dating sites bombard us with cause many of us to reduce the complex decision of finding the perfect match to good looks. Most likely, the doctor from our previous example would oversimplify, too. His main criteria would be not to risk a disturbance of his marriage. That is what would trick him into making the worse decision and keep smoking. His feelings have overruled his knowledge.

We make a similar mistake with many important decisions:

- We choose a safe career instead of the career we desire.
- We choose easily available friends instead of friends we have a lot in common with.
- We buy things to impress others instead of buying things we need.

In all three cases, the complexity of a decision tricks us into narrowing our criteria down to the most obvious characteristic. Knowing what we want in life is insufficient to guarantee that we pursue these things, we need a system that makes sure we do what we know is right. To solve this problem, there are decision-making models. These models can help us to:

- Make better decisions,
- Know which of many possible decisions is in line with our true selves, and
- Do what we know is right.

Let's take a look at what I consider to be the best decision-making model and how it can improve our lives. If you want to learn more about decision-making models, I recommend Mikael Krogerus' book *The Decision Book: Fifty Models of Strategic Thinking*. Which decision-making model works best for you depends on your character, but you are sure to find a good model in Krogerus' book.

Matrix analysis

The most effective system to avoid bad decisions is matrix analysis. Matrix analysis uses a coordinate system with value-based parameters & can make difficult decisions easier by visualizing them. It can put different options in perspective and show which is most in line with our values. When we decide which career to pursue, for example, we can create the happiest lives by using our talents to do what has intrinsic value to us. To decide which career combines these criteria the best, we can use intrinsic value and talent as parameters for our coordinate system and plot all possibilities along these axes. This coordinate system helps us understand all possible decisions. We can immediately understand which options are in line with our true selves and which are the result of false replacements. My coordinate system could look something like figure 1.

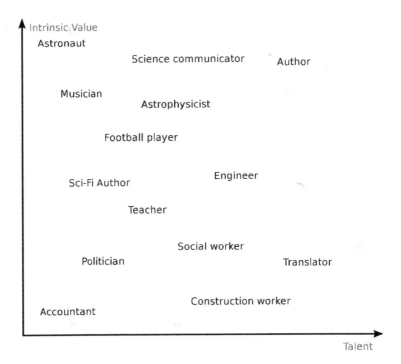

Figure 1

From this coordinate system, we can easily deduct which careers would be possible for me:

Intrinsic value?	Talent?	
yes	yes	Possible.
yes	no	High risk of failure, bad idea.
no	yes	Only possible if could add intrinsic value.
no	no	Not possible.

We can adapt this matrix to classify possible options in all aspects of life. To determine which tasks of our to-do list we should do first, we can plot how much a project helps us reach our goals against the x-axis and how much we can learn from a project against the y-axis. Our reaction to the different classifications could look something like this:

Intrinsic value?	Can learn from?	
yes	yes	Do it.
yes	no	Outsource it.
no	yes	Add intrinsic value or scrap it.
no	no	Scrap it.

We can use any set of parameters to visualize any decision. Make sure to choose parameters that help you live your true self.

Why self-help happiness techniques fail

The concepts presented in this chapter are fundamentally different from the happiness techniques promoted by self-help. Following its usual one-size-fits-all approach, self-help offers us concrete actions that are supposed to make us happy. Depending on whether they have intrinsic value to us or not, these actions might work for some of us - but they will fail for others. The techniques in this chapter are open and lead us to a decision that is individually right for us – an essential key to producing positive results.

One of the most suggested happiness techniques is performing acts of gratitude. Expressing thanks to our partners, parents, and loved ones, so goes the theory, will help us understand how much we have to be thankful for, thereby making us happier. If acts of gratitude have intrinsic value to us, this technique will indeed work and make us happier. If we lack things to be grateful for or if we have already expressed our gratitude, forcing this strategy means doing something extrinsic, making us unhappy.

Accordingly, studies that asked their subjects to write gratitude letters found that, on average, people in some countries became happier while people in other countries became less happy. This effect seems to be due to cultural differences. In some Asian cultures, it is considered an insult when children thank their parents for supporting them – it implies that the parents do their job reluctantly. To people with this cultural background, performing acts of gratitude towards their parents has no intrinsic value. They have a different super-ego and require different happiness strategies. For them, using this strategy will generate shame and false replacements.

We are all different and must follow our own paths to happiness. It is impossible to create a happiness technique that works for all of us. We can, however, replace all happiness techniques by the simple rule to do what has intrinsic value to us and to avoid what has only extrinsic value.

We can lead happier lives by focusing on techniques that help us make better decisions and avoid faulty logic. These techniques point us towards what has intrinsic value to us and eliminate everything else from our lives, providing us with a more effective strategy than the happiness techniques self-help books promote.

Self-Help Deception #40: There are happiness techniques that work for all of us.

Conclusion

1. Our mental processes are error prone. Making decisions that are in line with what we believe in is difficult.
2. There are patterns of faulty logic. These are always a false replacement of some kind.
3. It is hard to avoid faulty logic completely, but we can greatly reduce its influence by living our true selves. Decision-making models can help us with this process.

Further reading

Rolf Dobelli: The Art of Acting Clearly.
Similar to Dobelli's first book (mentioned in chapter 1), *The Art of Thinking Clearly* details more examples of faulty logic and how we can avoid them.

Mikael Krogerus: The Decision Book.
A good book full of strategies that help us understand what we want and which actions fit our needs.

Bidget M. Law: Seared in Our Memories, Monitor on Psychology 42, no. 8, 60-65.

An interesting article detailing the inaccuracy of our memories, especially of so-called light bulb memories which most people claim to be completely accurate.

Conclusion

"The unexamined life is not worth living."

SOCRATES

When I was 17 years old, I broke my neck in a car accident. I was revived twice, suffered brain injuries, had to learn to move my left arm again, and lost roughly 50 pounds. Over the next weeks and months, as I was trying to find my way back to the life I had lived before, something unexpected happened to me. While I enjoyed getting back to some of the activities, some didn't seem worth the effort. Before the accident, fear, insecurity, and the need for approval had tricked me into creating a life based on extrinsic activities – activities that didn't make me happy and added no value to my life. Now, forced into a new perspective on my old life, I suddenly realized how much these activities weighed on me. Nonetheless, eliminating them was more difficult than I had expected. Regardless of how hard I tried, I couldn't let go of the only ways I knew to satisfy my essential needs. The next years were a constant struggle to identify and eliminate what added no value to my life. I had to grow and find new, better ways to satisfy my needs – a challenging and scary process, but also a process that helped me break the chains I had enslaved myself in.

Roughly seven years later, as my disenchantment with self-help literature grew, and I started to read scientific research on happiness, my cleansing process was still far from complete. Up to that point, I had created a new false replacement as soon as I had eliminated an old one. While I will probably never be able to eliminate all false replacements from my life, every false replacement that I managed to eliminate helped me live a happier, calmer, and more fulfilled life:

- I finally understood the true motives behind my extrinsic activities, why I created them, and why they made me unhappy.
- I went from moving from one false replacement to the next towards a life based on what had intrinsic value to me.
- I eliminated all the activities and people from my life that only drained my happiness.

We could all profit from a similar cleansing process. While none of us will ever be able to eliminate all our false replacements and fighting false replacements will remain a lifelong battle, every little victory can increase our quality of life. The goal is not to eliminate false replacements completely – trying to do the impossible will cause failure, shame, and more false replacements. The goal is to minimize the negative influence false replacements have on our lives, especially when it comes to important decisions on love, finances, politics, faith, and health. When we free ourselves from our false replacements, we gain the power to move forward and pursue the things that matter most to us.

Many of us are hoping for happiness in the future. We think that we will be happy when we get a better job, make more money, or find a better relationship. Others dread what happened in the past and what could happen in the future. As we have seen in this book, neither approach can create a good life. No relationship, no job, and no amount of money will bring us happiness, and no end of a relationship, no job loss, and no disease – not even the death of a loved one – will create everlasting misery. Life's turning points are opportunities to learn and grow, to develop a complex character, and to cleanse ourselves from our false replacements. Understanding this connection helps us to become better, happier, and more capable versions of ourselves with every turning point we encounter.

When we fail to recognize how little our life circumstances influence our long-term happiness, we make our lives worse:

- We might enter a relationship or a new job with unrealistic expectations of how happy it can make us, setting us up for inevitable disappointment.
- We might leave perfectly good relationships and rewarding jobs, only to find that we were chasing an idealized, non-existent dream.
- We might overestimate the negative impact of ending a relationship, losing a job, or other life events such as our fleeting youth, which can throw us into depression or trick us into remaining in a bad job, relationship, etc.

Self-help propagates the idea that the quality of our lives depends on the height of our achievements, continually urging us to pursue more material wealth, better careers, and better relationships, implying that these things will make us happy. When we achieve one goal, we are supposed to switch to the next goal seamlessly, never satisfied, never happy, and never fulfilled. With this advice, self-help leads us to empty, unhappy, and unfulfilled lives. We will inevitably realize that we have reduced our lives to a continuous pursuit of empty goals and feel disappointed and ashamed. This shame tricks us into abandoning what has intrinsic value to us and creates false replacements. We can lead better, happier lives when we reduce the amount of shame we feel to a minimum, which means that we have to abandon the basic premise of self-help. While there are many factors that influence how much shame we feel, the most significant improvement we can make is to live our true selves. Living our true selves is the closest thing to a magic bullet for happiness, success, and fulfillment that an honest book can ever advise. When we do what has intrinsic value to us, we automatically avoid misleading ideas; we put our talents to their best use, and we are happy.

Instead of trying to conquer the world, we can create much happier lives by conquering ourselves. Happiness is found within, not without. Even without life-threatening injuries or a deep inner void, we can increase the quality of our lives by taking a step back, analyzing our actions, and questioning our motives. The resulting insights will inevitably point us toward a few of our false replacements. Eliminating these false replacements starts the journey to our true selves, to the things we truly desire.

Why we do something is more important than what it can get us. When we do what has intrinsic value to us, we are happier, more successful, and more fulfilled. At the same time, we benefit society because we put our energy to the best use. Happiness is something we can only generate ourselves, which is why we can obtain it immediately. Explaining this connection was the first goal of this book. The second goal was to explain the processes that trick us into lives that fail to make us happy. All of these processes are related to shame. When we subscribe to misguided ideas and ideologies, when we try to do what we are incapable of doing, and when we overestimate ourselves, we inevitably fail and feel shame. To deal with this shame, we create false replacements. False replacements do not work, so we feel more shame.

Self-help propagates unreflective ideologies that push us all in one direction, regardless of whether this direction is right for us or not. For someone like me, who grew up in a post-socialist society where four decades of telling people that they ought to be ashamed of who they are and they shouldn't think for themselves caused this way of thinking to be forced on us, too, self-help was an initially positive tool that helped me to evaluate myself more realistically and accept my strengths. If you undervalue yourself, you will profit from self-help's teachings, too – at first. After a while, however, when you have reached the point of realistic self-evaluation, self-help will keep pushing you to more self-esteem, to higher pursuits. By the principle that if a little was good more has to be better, we are likely to stick with what has worked for us in the past, even though it is no longer able to improve our lives, getting us into situations where we can only fail. For the majority of us whom the self-serving bias has tricked into overvaluing ourselves, self-help will have a destructive influence from the start. Regardless of which group we belong to, we can all profit from employing a philosophy of life that helps us evaluate ourselves as realistically as possible.

Self-help exploits our search for happiness and a better life, our desire for quick ways to solve our problems. By always searching for the one idea that can eliminate all our problems we ignore the one power we truly have: to create good lives by using our strengths to contribute to the values we are passionate about. The answer to all our questions lies within us. If we need help, we are better off trusting the support system around us - our friends, our family, and our community – than wasting our hard earned money on self-help, life coaching, or gurus.

Most of us live in free societies that allow us to become anything we want. These societies offer us ideal conditions to lead good, happy lives. Unfortunately, our inner mental processes can easily trick us into wasting this opportunity and enslave us to shame, fear, and insecurity. The two cleansing processes of my life took roughly ten years altogether, but it was the most rewarding journey imaginable. I hope this book will guide you to a similarly rewarding journey and free you from the misleading ideas that self-help and other destructive ideas have propagated.

Thank you for reading this book.

Ten rules for a good, happy life

Many self-help books leave their readers without a concrete concept to take away. To do a better job, here are ten rules for a good, happy life. Please understand that these rules are an attempt to simplify this book's message into ten short rules – an attempt that inevitably borders on oversimplification. To give you something to hold on to, I will take this risk, but please refrain from making these ten rules the only part of the book you read. I strongly encourage you to take a look at the chapters that explain the reasoning behind these rules and the nuances by which they apply to our lives. Understanding how we arrived at a rule is more important than the rule itself.

1. Instead of subscribing to some magic formula, idea, or ideology for success and happiness, find your own path.
   Our world is too complex and too unpredictable to force great success by applying a magic concept, as self-help suggests. When we try, we set ourselves up for failure and disappointment. Since we are all genetically unique, and the myth that we can become anything we want has been disproven, we need to recognize our genetic strengths and passions and make the most of them.

2. To find your own path, use passion to develop your talents into skills and then use your skills to contribute to the values you are passionate about. Focus on what you can contribute over what you get.
   Long term happiness is the result of contribution and growth. No change of life circumstances, positive or negative, will make us as happy as the things that we contribute and the personal growth we experience along the way.

3. Never be ashamed of who you are.
   When you face an inner conflict between your desires and your conscience, resolve this conflict constructively by combining both without suppressing either part. Suppressing a part of who we are always makes us feel ashamed and creates false replacements.

4. Avoid doing what has no intrinsic value to you.
   It makes you unhappy and creates false replacements. If an extrinsic task is unavoidable, integrate it into what has intrinsic value to you.

5. Think of the pursuit of happiness more as a subtraction process than an addition process.
   Most of us in the first world have enough to sustain the standard of living that we need to be happy. We can find happiness by eliminating our false replacements and living our true selves, not by adding possessions, relationships, or achievements.

6. Find a way to make enough money to sustain the lifestyle you desire.
   If you make more money than you need, do not expand your standard of living, or you will enslave yourself to things that do not contribute to your quality of life. Rather

donate the excess money or find a way to use it to contribute to the values you are passionate about.

7. Evaluate yourself as reasonably as possible and convey the most realistic image of yourself to others that you can. Accept that you can't do everything, that you do not know everything, that you can't control everything, and that you can't be happy all the time.
   If you aren't satisfied with the image you convey, change your life, do not manipulate your image.

8. Never believe any concept, ideology, or idea that tells you that you are special, deserve preferential treatment, or should be ashamed of who you are, or any concept that divides humans into groups.
   These ideas are always false replacements. Building our lives around them sets us up for failure, shame, and unhappiness.

9. Never hurt anybody or their property.
   The true self is peaceful. It wants to benefit, not destroy. Even when someone attacks us, the true self wants to stop the threat in a way that helps the aggressor solve his problems, too. When we get angry at someone, we are dealing with a false replacement.

10. Never accept any idea that is based on wishful thinking and not on scientific evidence, critical thinking, and hard facts.
    Only the scientific method, the search for disconfirming evidence, can find the truth. Anything else will lead us to misconception, failure, and shame, creating false replacements and destroying our lives.

ABOUT THE AUTHOR

Chris Masi is an independent science, psychology, and philosophy writer. He received master degrees in political science and modern history from the University of Jena and has spent a lifetime studying psychology, philosophy, and self-help. For more information, visit his blog at www.chrismasi.net.

ACKNOWLEDGEMENTS

I can't thank my editor David Duncan enough. After reading the first version of this book, David volunteered to edit it for free. With his gift of using small changes to make a big difference, he elevated my writing to a level I would have been unable to reach on my own. Thank you for your commitment, the final result is as much your work as it is mine. You are a truly special person.

I would also like to thank my test readers B. Schoder, S. Schulz, and M. Kästner. With your input, you helped me to create a much better book than I could have written without you.

One final request

Dear reader,

If you liked this book, I would greatly appreciate it if you write a short, honest review of it on Amazon. For self-published authors, these reviews are the lifeblood of our careers. They help a book rank higher in the search results and show other readers that this book has valuable content. If you enjoyed reading this book, please help me out and help other readers find this book by leaving a review.

Thank you very much,

Chris

Image Sources

Made in the USA
Middletown, DE
26 September 2017